GALVESTON DIET
COOKBOOK FOR BEGINNERS

*Your Fast-Track to Hormone Balance and Lasting Fat Loss
with Simple, Anti-Inflammatory Recipes*

By

ANGELA VEGA

CONTENTS

PART II: GALVESTON DIET RECIPES

PART III: GALVESTON DIET LIFESTYLE

INTRODUCTION

Welcome to the world of the Galveston Diet, a revolutionary approach to eating that transcends the conventional goals of mere weight loss. This diet centers on achieving a delicate hormonal balance, reducing inflammation, and fostering a lifestyle that significantly enhances your overall well-being. As someone who has navigated this path, I can vouch for the transformative effects it can have not just on your physical health, but also on your emotional and mental states.

In this guide, we will understand the essence of what makes the Galveston Diet truly unique, unpacking its foundational principles and illustrating why it might be the exact change you've been seeking for your dietary needs. Whether you're navigating through midlife hormonal shifts, struggling with stubborn weight, or simply in pursuit of a healthier lifestyle, this book is designed to equip you with the necessary knowledge and tools to seamlessly integrate this diet into your life.

PART I:

UNDERSTANDING THE GALVESTON DIET

CHAPTER 1:
What is the Galveston Diet?

The Galveston Diet is the innovative creation of Dr. Mary Claire Haver, a gynecologist and an expert in women's health. Recognizing the unique dietary needs of women experiencing menopause, including the common issues of hormonal imbalances and weight gain, Dr. Haver crafted a dietary program tailored to address these specific challenges. However, the benefits of the diet have shown to be universally advantageous, making it a suitable choice for anyone looking to enhance their health through thoughtful, informed dietary choices.

This diet is founded on three pivotal components: the incorporation of anti-inflammatory foods, the strategic use of intermittent fasting, and a keen focus on maintaining a balance of macronutrients to optimize hormonal function. Contrary to many diets that impose restrictive eating patterns, the Galveston Diet promotes a sustainable and enjoyable way of eating that encourages health without deprivation.

OVERVIEW AND ORIGINS

The origins of the Galveston Diet are deeply personal to its founder. Dr. Haver's own encounter with menopausal weight gain and the noticeable absence of effective dietary solutions targeting the hormonal upheavals during this life phase inspired her to develop this specialized program. Her approach goes beyond mere weight management, aiming to alleviate the array of discomforts triggered by hormonal fluctuations.

Named after the city where Dr. Haver first practiced and implemented these dietary principles, Galveston, Texas, the diet has since cultivated a respected reputation. Its scientific foundation and health-promoting benefits have attracted a growing following, not only among her own patients but also among a broad demographic seeking a lifestyle oriented towards genuine health improvement.

HOW IT DIFFERS FROM OTHER DIETS

A Focus on Anti-Inflammatory Foods

At its core, the Galveston Diet prioritizes foods known for their anti-inflammatory properties. Chronic inflammation has been linked to a host of health issues, including but not limited to cardiovascular diseases, diabetes, and various forms of cancer. By emphasizing foods rich in antioxidants and phytochemicals, this diet goes a long way in combatting inflammation and bolstering the body's overall health.

Hormonal Balance Through Diet

One of the standout features of the Galveston Diet is its emphasis on foods that aid in regulating hormones. Foods rich in omega-3 fatty acids, along with those containing phytoestrogens, play a crucial role in stabilizing hormone levels, which can be particularly volatile during periods like menopause or even regular menstrual cycles. This strategic focus helps in mitigating the physical and emotional symptoms associated with hormonal imbalance.

The Role of Intermittent Fasting

Intermittent fasting is another cornerstone of the Galveston Diet, praised for its ability to enhance insulin sensitivity and improve overall hormonal function. However, the approach here transcends the typical focus on weight loss seen in other fasting protocols. It's about giving your body the time it needs to heal and rejuvenate, highlighting the restorative aspects of fasting rather than its potential for rapid weight loss.

Long-term Sustainability

Unlike many diets that target quick results through drastic means, the Galveston Diet promotes enduring lifestyle changes. This approach encourages individuals to adopt a way of eating that can be sustained over a lifetime, thus fostering lasting health benefits without the cyclical patterns of weight loss and gain that characterize many diets.

Grounded in Science

Every aspect of the Galveston Diet is underpinned by rigorous scientific research, particularly in areas related to nutritional biochemistry and hormonal health. This strong scientific basis provides followers with the reassurance that the benefits of the diet extend beyond anecdotal evidence, offering a solid foundation for the positive changes they experience.

The Galveston Diet is more than a set of nutritional guidelines; it is a new way to look at food and its impact on our bodies. As you will see throughout this book, the focus is always on nourishing the body, supporting hormonal health, and reducing inflammation through delicious, whole foods. This approach not only helps in managing weight but also plays a crucial role in overall health maintenance, making you feel revitalized and rebalanced.

As we venture further into the mechanics and practical applications of the Galveston Diet in subsequent chapters, you will gain deeper insights into how these principles can be adapted into your daily routine. This guide aims to empower you with comprehensive knowledge and practical strategies, enhancing your ability to make informed dietary choices that will profoundly impact your health and well-being. Let's begin this enlightening path together, equipped with the right tools and insights to make the transition both enjoyable and profoundly beneficial.

CHAPTER 2:
Fundamental Concepts of the Galveston Diet

he Galveston Diet has captured the attention of many looking for a sustainable way to manage health, particularly as it pertains to inflammation, hormonal balance, and overall nutritional well-being. This diet isn't just a fad or a quick fix; it's a comprehensive approach to eating that considers the long-term impacts of dietary choices on the body. In this chapter, we will explore the three fundamental concepts that form the pillars of the Galveston Diet: Hormonal Health, Anti-Inflammatory Eating, and Nutrient Density. Each of these components plays a crucial role in how the diet functions and benefits its followers.

HORMONAL HEALTH

Hormones are powerful chemicals that influence virtually every aspect of our health. From metabolic processes to mood regulation, maintaining hormonal balance is key to achieving and sustaining optimal health. The Galveston Diet recognizes this importance and strategically focuses on foods and eating patterns that support endocrine health.

Understanding Hormonal Imbalances

Hormonal imbalances can disrupt metabolic functions, leading to weight gain, fatigue, and a host of other health issues. For women, especially those entering or experiencing menopause, these imbalances can be particularly challenging. The decline in estrogen and progesterone can affect everything from bone density to heart health. The Galveston Diet addresses these changes head-on by incorporating foods that help stabilize hormone levels naturally.

Foods That Promote Hormonal Balance

Foods rich in omega-3 fatty acids, such as salmon and flaxseeds, are emphasized for their anti-inflammatory properties and their role in hormone production. Phytoestrogens found in foods like soy and flax can mimic the effects of estrogen in the body, helping to balance hormone levels. Additionally, cruciferous vegetables like broccoli and kale support liver function and aid in the detoxification of excess hormones.

The diet also recommends moderate, regular consumption of healthy fats from avocados, nuts, and seeds, which are crucial for hormone synthesis. By maintaining a balanced intake of these nutrients, the Galveston Diet helps streamline hormonal functions, assisting in everything from weight management to mood stabilization.

ANTI-INFLAMMATORY EATING

Chronic inflammation is a root cause of many diseases, including heart disease, diabetes, and cancer. The Galveston Diet's strong emphasis on anti-inflammatory eating is designed not only to prevent disease but also to enhance daily vitality and reduce the risk of chronic health conditions.

The Role of Inflammation in Disease

Inflammation is the body's natural response to injury or infection, a crucial part of the healing process. However, when inflammation becomes chronic, it can lead to cellular damage and a variety of long-term health issues. Diet plays a significant role in either exacerbating or reducing inflammation.

Anti-Inflammatory Foods

The Galveston Diet includes a plethora of anti-inflammatory foods that help mitigate the inflammatory process and promote better health. Turmeric, with its active component curcumin, has been shown to have powerful anti-inflammatory effects. Ginger, green tea, and fatty fish are also integral to the diet, known for their anti-inflammatory properties.

Fruits and vegetables are loaded with antioxidants that combat oxidative stress, a key contributor to inflammation. The diet encourages the consumption of colorful produce to ensure a wide range of antioxidants and phytonutrients. Additionally, whole grains and fiber-rich foods are included to support digestive health and reduce inflammation.

NUTRIENT DENSITY

To maximize health benefits, the Galveston Diet focuses on nutrient density, which refers to the amount of beneficial nutrients in a food relative to its calorie content. This concept is fundamental to the diet's effectiveness, as it ensures each calorie consumed is also delivering vitamins, minerals, and other essential nutrients that support overall health.

Importance of Nutrient-Dense Foods

Consuming nutrient-dense foods allows for more efficient calorie use, meaning the body can obtain all the necessary nutrients without excess energy intake, which can lead to weight gain. This is particularly beneficial for metabolic health and can help manage and prevent conditions such as type 2 diabetes and obesity.

Examples of Nutrient-Dense Foods

Leafy greens, such as spinach and kale, top the list of nutrient-dense foods, offering high levels of vitamins and minerals with very few calories. Berries are another excellent choice, packed with vitamins, minerals, and antioxidants, while being relatively low in calories. Lean proteins, whole grains, and legumes also feature prominently in the Galveston Diet, providing balanced nutrients that support sustained energy levels and overall health.

Incorporating a variety of these foods into your diet ensures that your body receives a spectrum of nutrients necessary for maintaining health and preventing disease. The focus on whole, minimally processed foods maximizes nutrient intake and supports the body's natural processes, from immune function to cell repair.

It's clear that the Galveston Diet is more than just a means to lose weight. It's a holistic approach to eating that considers the long-term effects of diet on hormonal health, inflammation, and nutrient intake. By following the principles outlined here, you can ensure that you're not only managing your weight but also improving your overall health, setting the stage for a healthier, more vibrant life.

CHAPTER 3:
The Galveston Approach to Hormonal Balance

The Galveston Diet is not just another trend in the world of health and nutrition; it is a scientifically backed, holistic approach to managing your health through the foods you eat, with a particular focus on hormonal balance. Hormones control virtually every aspect of our health, from how we feel to how we metabolize food. As we age, our hormonal landscape shifts, especially during critical periods such as menopause. This chapter will explore how the Galveston Diet influences hormones and provides strategic support through these transitions, offering a sustainable path to wellness.

Nutritional Support for Hormonal Health

The Galveston Diet focuses on nutrients that are pivotal for hormone production and regulation. These include fats, proteins, and certain minerals and vitamins that are essential for the synthesis and balance of hormones like estrogen, progesterone, and testosterone. For instance, fats are not merely sources of energy; they are critical for building cellular structures and producing hormones. The diet emphasizes healthy fats from sources like fish, nuts, and seeds, which provide omega-3 fatty acids known to support hormonal health and reduce inflammation.

Proteins, on the other hand, are crucial for the repair and creation of new cells, including those involved in hormonal pathways. The Galveston Diet recommends high-quality protein sources, such as lean meats, fish, and legumes, which help stabilize blood sugar levels and support the adrenal glands, thus indirectly supporting hormone regulation.

MANAGING MENOPAUSE AND MIDLIFE HORMONAL CHANGES

Menopause is a significant hormonal transition for women, often accompanied by symptoms like hot flashes, weight gain, and mood swings. These changes can be challenging, but the Galveston Diet provides a framework for easing these symptoms through targeted nutritional strategies.

Diet and Menopause Symptom Management

The fluctuations in estrogen and progesterone during menopause can affect your metabolic rate and how your body stores fat. The Galveston Diet addresses these changes by encouraging foods that can help manage weight and balance hormones. Phytoestrogen-rich foods such as flax seeds and soy products can mimic the effects of estrogen in the body, helping to moderate symptoms associated with estrogen deficiency.

Furthermore, the diet's low-glycemic approach helps stabilize blood sugar levels, which can fluctuate more dramatically during menopause. By avoiding high-sugar and refined-carbohydrate foods, women following the Galveston Diet can manage cravings and mood swings, maintain energy levels, and prevent menopause-related weight gain.

Importance of Nutrient Density During Menopause

As women age, the need for nutrient-dense foods becomes even more critical. The Galveston Diet prioritizes foods that are high in vitamins and minerals necessary for maintaining bone density, such as calcium, magnesium, and vitamin D. These nutrients are vital during menopause, as the decrease in estrogen levels can lead to bone loss.

Incorporating a variety of vegetables, fruits, whole grains, and lean proteins ensures that the body gets a comprehensive spectrum of nutrients needed to support overall health and well-being during midlife. This approach not only helps in managing the physical aspects of menopause but also supports cognitive function and emotional health.

As we wrap up this discussion on the Galveston Diet and its approach to hormonal balance, it's clear that this diet is more than just a set of eating guidelines. It's a comprehensive lifestyle approach that uses the power of nutrition to support hormonal health at every stage of life, but particularly during the critical periods of change such as menopause. By following the principles of the Galveston Diet, you can help ensure that your body has the tools it needs to manage these changes effectively and maintain a balanced, healthy life.

CHAPTER 4:
Intermittent Fasting the Galveston Way

I ntermittent fasting has gained widespread attention for its potential health benefits, ranging from improved metabolic rates to enhanced longevity. The Galveston Diet incorporates intermittent fasting not as a trend, but as a fundamental component to support hormonal balance and metabolic health. This chapter explores how intermittent fasting is integrated into the Galveston Diet and the specific benefits it brings, especially concerning hormonal regulation and metabolic efficiency.

INTEGRATING INTERMITTENT FASTING WITH THE GALVESTON DIET

The Galveston Diet uses intermittent fasting as a tool to complement its focus on anti-inflammatory foods and hormonal balance. The approach is not about depriving oneself but about creating space for the body to renew and repair itself. Let's look at how intermittent fasting is structured within the context of the Galveston Diet.

The Fasting Schedule

The most common method of intermittent fasting under the Galveston Diet involves the 16/8 approach, where you eat all your day's meals within an eight-hour window and fast for the remaining 16 hours. This schedule is flexible depending on individual lifestyles, but it generally means skipping breakfast and eating the first meal at noon and the last meal by 8 PM. This timing aligns well with natural circadian rhythms, supporting metabolic health and energy levels.

Making the Most of the Eating Window

During the eating window, the focus is on consuming nutrient-dense, anti-inflammatory foods that support hormonal balance. Meals are composed of a balance of macronutrients—healthy fats, proteins, and carbohydrates—in proportions that sustain energy and satiety without overindulgence. The idea is to eat until you are satisfied but not stuffed, using the principles of mindful eating.

Support and Adaptability

For beginners, the transition to intermittent fasting can be eased into gradually. Starting with a shorter fasting period, such as 12 hours, and increasing the fasting window as the body adapts, helps make the process more manageable. The Galveston Diet emphasizes listening to your body and adjusting the fasting schedule as needed to fit individual health needs and lifestyle constraints.

BENEFITS FOR METABOLISM AND HORMONAL BALANCE SPECIFIC TO THE DIET

Intermittent fasting within the Galveston Diet framework brings specific benefits, particularly for metabolism and hormonal health. Understanding these benefits can help clarify why this approach is so central to the diet's philosophy.

Enhancing Metabolic Flexibility

Metabolic flexibility is the body's ability to switch between burning carbohydrates and fats efficiently. Intermittent fasting improves this flexibility by allowing the body time to deplete glycogen stores and start mobilizing fat as a fuel source. This not only aids in weight management but also enhances energy levels and endurance. By training the body to utilize its fuel sources more efficiently, intermittent fasting can help stabilize blood sugar levels, reduce insulin resistance, and decrease the risk of type 2 diabetes.

Regulating Hormone Levels

Intermittent fasting impacts several key hormones related to hunger and satiety, including insulin, leptin, and ghrelin. By normalizing insulin levels during the fasting periods, the diet helps prevent insulin spikes and crashes that can lead to cravings and overeating. Additionally, fasting has been shown to increase leptin sensitivity, which helps regulate fat storage and hunger signals, and decrease ghrelin levels, often referred to as the "hunger hormone."

Supporting Hormonal Health During Menopause

For women, particularly those going through menopause, intermittent fasting can offer specific benefits by helping manage the hormonal fluctuations that accompany this stage. The stress on the body from constant eating can exacerbate hormonal imbalances, so providing longer periods between meals allows the body to stabilize these hormones naturally. Furthermore, the reduction in insulin resistance through intermittent fasting can help manage the weight gain often associated with menopausal changes.

Detoxification and Cellular Repair

The periods of fasting activate pathways in the body that promote cellular repair processes, such as the removal of waste material from cells, a process known as autophagy. This not only contributes to better cellular health and function but also enhances the body's ability to fight aging and development of diseases. The detoxification process during fasting periods also supports liver health, which is crucial for hormone processing and balance.

It's clear that this practice is not just a supplementary aspect of the diet—it's a core element that enhances the diet's overall effectiveness. By understanding and implementing these fasting strategies, individuals can experience profound benefits not just in terms of weight management, but also in overall health improvement, particularly in the areas of metabolic health and hormonal balance. Embracing this approach allows you to support your body in its natural rhythms and healing processes, leading to a more vibrant and healthier life.

CHAPTER 5:
Mastering Anti-Inflammatory Eating with the Galveston Diet

The cornerstone of achieving and maintaining good health can often be found in the ability to control inflammation through diet. The Galveston Diet, with its strong emphasis on reducing inflammation, offers a practical and effective approach to eating that not only combats inflammation but also enhances overall wellness. This chapter delves into the principles of anti-inflammatory eating as prescribed by the Galveston Diet, focusing on specific foods to emphasize and how to create meals that support holistic health.

ANTI-INFLAMMATORY FOODS TO EMPHASIZE ON THE GALVESTON DIET

Inflammation is a natural immune response, but when it becomes chronic, it can lead to a host of health issues, including heart disease, arthritis, and even depression. The Galveston Diet strategically incorporates foods known for their anti-inflammatory properties to help mitigate these risks.

Fatty Fish

Rich in omega-3 fatty acids, fatty fish like salmon, mackerel, and sardines are champions in the fight against inflammation. Omega-3s are known to reduce the levels of inflammatory eicosanoids and cytokines, which are biochemical markers of inflammation. Incorporating two to three servings of fatty fish per week can significantly lower the risk of chronic diseases associated with inflammation.

Leafy Greens

Vegetables such as spinach, kale, and Swiss chard are high in vitamins and minerals like folate and magnesium, which are crucial for reducing inflammation. These leafy greens also contain high levels of antioxidants that help neutralize harmful free radicals in the body.

Nuts and Seeds

Almonds, walnuts, flaxseeds, and chia seeds are not only great sources of healthy fats but also contain fiber, protein, and antioxidants. The fats in nuts are primarily anti-inflammatory omega-3 fatty acids, which help reduce inflammation throughout the body.

Berries

Berries are small but mighty sources of antioxidants, particularly anthocyanins, which have pronounced anti-inflammatory effects. Blueberries, strawberries, raspberries, and blackberries can be a delicious way to fight inflammation.

Olive Oil

A staple in the Mediterranean diet, which is renowned for its health benefits, olive oil is rich in oleocanthal, an antioxidant that has been shown to work similarly to anti-inflammatory drugs like ibuprofen.

Turmeric and Ginger

These spices are famous for their anti-inflammatory properties. Turmeric contains curcumin, a compound that inhibits inflammation at the molecular level. Ginger, similarly, can reduce inflammation related to arthritis and other conditions.

CREATING MEALS THAT COMBAT INFLAMMATION AND SUPPORT OVERALL HEALTH

Understanding which foods to include is just the first step; learning how to combine these into daily meals is where the Galveston Diet excels, providing a sustainable method to manage and reduce inflammation through diet.

Start with a Solid Base

Every meal should start with a solid base of vegetables, whether it's a leafy green salad, a medley of steamed vegetables, or a vibrant vegetable stir-fry. This ensures you're getting a substantial amount of antioxidants and phytonutrients, which are essential for reducing inflammation and supporting overall health.

Incorporate Protein

Choose lean protein sources that complement the anti-inflammatory nature of your meal. Options like grilled salmon, baked chicken breast, or even plant-based proteins like lentils and chickpeas can help build and repair body tissues without adding inflammatory elements to your diet.

Add Healthy Fats

Incorporate a source of healthy fats into each meal. This could be drizzling olive oil over a salad, adding avocado to a sandwich, or mixing nuts and seeds into a morning oatmeal. Healthy fats help absorb fat-soluble vitamins and are vital for reducing inflammation.

Spice It Up

Utilize herbs and spices not only to flavor your dishes but also to boost their health properties. Adding turmeric to your curry, ginger to your tea, or basil to your pasta can enhance the anti-inflammatory capacity of your meals.

Hydration

Finally, proper hydration is crucial for maintaining cellular health and assisting in the reduction of inflammation. Water helps flush toxins from the body and keeps your cells in top working order. Herbal teas, such as green tea or ginger tea, can also be beneficial due to their antioxidant properties.

By following the Galveston Diet's guidelines for anti-inflammatory eating, you equip your body with the necessary tools to fight inflammation and promote lasting health. Each meal becomes an opportunity to nourish your body and protect it from the chronic inflammation that can lead to disease. With these principles in mind, you can enjoy delicious, healthful meals that support your well-being every day.

PART II:

GALVESTON DIET RECIPES

CHAPTER 6:
Breakfast Recipes

SMOOTHIES: BLENDS THAT BALANCE HORMONES

Avocado and Berry Smoothie

Servings: 2
Prep Time: 5 minutes
Cook Time: 0 minutes

Ingredients:
1. 1 avocado (200g)
2. 1 cup mixed berries, frozen (150g)
3. 1 1/2 cups unsweetened almond milk (360ml)
4. 2 tablespoons honey (40g)
5. Ice cubes

Instructions:
6. Place the avocado, mixed berries, almond milk, honey, and a handful of ice cubes into a blender.
7. Blend on high until the mixture is smooth and creamy.
8. Pour into two glasses and serve immediately.

Nutritional Information: Kcal: 320, Cho: 44g, Fat: 15g, Na: 60mg, Pro: 3g

Spinach, Flaxseed, and Blueberry Smoothie

Servings: 2
Prep Time: 5 minutes
Cook Time: 0 minutes

Ingredients:

1. 2 cups fresh spinach (60g)
2. 2 tablespoons ground flaxseed (14g)
3. 1 cup blueberries, frozen (150g)
4. 1 1/2 cups unsweetened almond milk (360ml)
5. 2 teaspoons honey (14g)

Instructions:

6. Combine the spinach, ground flaxseed, blueberries, almond milk, and honey in a blender.
7. Blend until the smoothie is smooth and even.
8. Divide the smoothie between two glasses and serve.

Nutritional Information: Kcal: 190, Cho: 30g, Fat: 7g, Na: 60mg, Pro: 5g

Almond Butter and Banana Smoothie

Servings: 2
Prep Time: 5 minutes
Cook Time: 0 minutes

Ingredients:

1. 2 ripe bananas (236g)
2. 2 tablespoons almond butter (32g)
3. 1 1/2 cups unsweetened almond milk (360ml)
4. 1 teaspoon vanilla extract (5ml)
5. Ice cubes

Instructions:

6. Add the bananas, almond butter, almond milk, vanilla extract, and a few ice cubes to a blender.
7. Blend until smooth and frothy.
8. Pour the smoothie into two glasses and enjoy.

Nutritional Information: Kcal: 385, Cho: 53g, Fat: 17g, Na: 90mg, Pro: 8g

Cucumber, Kale, and Apple Smoothie

Servings: 2
Prep Time: 5 minutes
Cook Time: 0 minutes

Ingredients:

1. 1 cucumber, sliced (240g)
2. 2 cups kale, chopped (134g)
3. 2 small apples, cored and sliced (364g)
4. 2 cups water (480ml)
5. Juice of 1 lemon (44ml)

Instructions:

6. Prepare all ingredients and place them in the blender.
7. Add the water and lemon juice.
8. Blend until completely smooth.
9. Serve the smoothie immediately, chilled.

Nutritional Information: Kcal: 180, Cho: 46g, Fat: 1g, Na: 30mg, Pro: 4g

Chia Seed and Peach Smoothie

Servings: 2
Prep Time: 10 minutes (includes soaking time)
Cook Time: 0 minutes

Ingredients:

1. 4 tablespoons chia seeds (56g)
2. 2 large peaches, sliced (300g)
3. 1 1/2 cups unsweetened almond milk (360ml)
4. 1 teaspoon ground cinnamon (2g)
5. Ice cubes

Instructions:

6. Soak the chia seeds in 1/2 cup of water (120ml) for about 10 minutes until they become gel-like.
7. In a blender, combine the soaked chia seeds, sliced peaches, almond milk, cinnamon, and a few ice cubes.
8. Blend until the mixture is smooth.
9. Pour into two glasses and serve immediately for a refreshing treat.

Nutritional Information: Kcal: 295, Cho: 45g, Fat: 12g, Na: 95mg, Pro: 8g

Coconut Water and Pineapple Smoothie

Servings: 2
Prep Time: 5 minutes
Cook Time: 0 minutes

Ingredients:

1. 2 cups coconut water (480ml)
2. 1 cup pineapple chunks, frozen (165g)
3. 1 banana (118g)
4. 1 tablespoon lime juice (15ml)

Instructions:

5. Place coconut water, frozen pineapple chunks, banana, and lime juice into a blender.
6. Blend until the mixture is smooth and frothy.
7. Pour the smoothie into two glasses and serve chilled.

Nutritional Information: Kcal: 160, Cho: 39g, Fat: 1g, Na: 252mg, Pro: 2g

Beetroot and Ginger Smoothie

Servings: 2
Prep Time: 10 minutes
Cook Time: 0 minutes

Ingredients:

1. 1 medium beetroot, peeled and chopped (170g)
2. 1 inch fresh ginger, peeled (15g)
3. 1 apple, cored and sliced (182g)
4. 1/2 lemon, juiced (22ml)
5. 1 cup water (240ml)

Instructions:

6. Add the chopped beetroot, ginger, apple slices, lemon juice, and water to a blender.
7. Blend on high until all components are thoroughly combined and the texture is smooth.
8. Divide the smoothie into two servings and enjoy the vibrant, energizing drink.

Nutritional Information: Kcal: 95, Cho: 23g, Fat: 0g, Na: 64mg, Pro: 2g

Celery and Green Apple Smoothie

Servings: 2
Prep Time: 5 minutes
Cook Time: 0 minutes

Servings: 2
Prep Time: 5 minutes
Cook Time: 0 minutes
Ingredients:
1. 4 stalks celery, chopped (160g)
2. 2 green apples, cored and chopped (364g)
3. 1 cup spinach leaves (30g)
4. 2 tablespoons lemon juice (30ml)
5. 1 cup water (240ml)

Instructions:
6. Combine celery, green apples, spinach, lemon juice, and water in the blender.
7. Blend until smooth, ensuring that all ingredients are fully integrated.
8. Serve the smoothie immediately, split between two glasses, for a refreshing and cleansing drink.

Nutritional Information: Kcal: 120, Cho: 30g, Fat: 1g, Na: 80mg, Pro: 2g

Carrot and Orange Boost

Servings: 2
Prep Time: 5 minutes
Cook Time: 0 minutes

Ingredients:
1. 4 large carrots, peeled and chopped (480g)
2. 2 oranges, peeled and segmented (280g)
3. 1 inch turmeric root, peeled (15g)
4. 1 tablespoon lemon juice (15ml)
5. 1 cup water (240ml)

Instructions:
6. Place carrots, orange segments, turmeric root, lemon juice, and water into your blender.
7. Secure the lid and blend on high until the mixture is completely smooth.
8. Pour into two glasses, offering a nutritious drink that's perfect for a morning or midday energy boost.

Nutritional Information: Kcal: 160, Cho: 38g, Fat: 1g, Na: 68mg, Pro: 3g

Turkey and Spinach Omelette

Servings: 2
Prep Time: 5 minutes
Cook Time: 10 minutes

Ingredients:

1. 4 eggs (200g)
2. 1/2 cup chopped cooked turkey breast (85g)
3. 1 cup fresh spinach, chopped (30g)
4. 1 tablespoon olive oil (15ml)
5. Salt and pepper to taste

Instructions:

6. In a bowl, whisk the eggs until smooth.
7. Heat olive oil in a skillet over medium heat (350°F or 177°C).
8. Sauté the spinach until wilted, about 2 minutes.
9. Add the chopped turkey to the skillet and warm through.
10. Pour the eggs over the spinach and turkey, season with salt and pepper, and cook until the eggs are set, about 6-7 minutes.
11. Fold the omelette in half and serve.

Nutritional Information: Kcal: 290, Cho: 2g, Fat: 20g, Na: 410mg, Pro: 27g

Greek Yogurt with Nuts and Honey

Servings: 2
Prep Time: 5 minutes
Cook Time: 0 minutes

Ingredients:

1. 2 cups Greek yogurt, non-fat (460g)
2. 2 tablespoons honey (40g)
3. 1/4 cup mixed nuts, chopped (30g)

Instructions:

4. Divide the Greek yogurt between two bowls.
5. Drizzle each serving with honey.
6. Sprinkle chopped nuts over the top.
7. Serve immediately for a refreshing and protein-rich breakfast or snack.

Nutritional Information: Kcal: 245, Cho: 28g, Fat: 6g, Na: 85mg, Pro: 20g

Cottage Cheese and Pineapple Bowl

Servings: 2
Prep Time: 5 minutes
Cook Time: 0 minutes

Ingredients:

1. 2 cups low-fat cottage cheese (460g)
2. 1 cup pineapple chunks (165g)

Instructions:

3. Divide the cottage cheese between two bowls.
4. Top each bowl with pineapple chunks.
5. Mix lightly and serve chilled as a sweet and tangy breakfast or snack.

Nutritional Information: Kcal: 230, Cho: 20g, Fat: 2g, Na: 500mg, Pro: 28g

Smoked Salmon and Avocado Toast

Servings: 2
Prep Time: 5 minutes
Cook Time: 5 minutes

Ingredients:

1. 4 slices whole-grain bread (120g)
2. 4 ounces smoked salmon (113g)
3. 1 avocado, sliced (200g)
4. 1 tablespoon lemon juice (15ml)
5. Salt and pepper to taste

Instructions:

6. Toast the bread slices until golden and crisp.
7. Mash the avocado with lemon juice, salt, and pepper.
8. Spread the avocado mixture evenly over each slice of toasted bread.
9. Top with smoked salmon.
10. Serve immediately for a nutritious and satisfying meal.

Nutritional Information: Kcal: 360, Cho: 33g, Fat: 17g, Na: 760mg, Pro: 23g

Scrambled Eggs with Sautéed Mushrooms

Servings: 2
Prep Time: 5 minutes
Cook Time: 10 minutes

Ingredients:

1. 4 eggs (200g)
2. 1 cup mushrooms, sliced (70g)
3. 1 tablespoon olive oil (15ml)
4. Salt and pepper to taste

Instructions:

5. Heat olive oil in a skillet over medium heat (350°F or 177°C).
6. Add the sliced mushrooms and sauté until tender and golden, about 5 minutes.
7. In a bowl, whisk the eggs and season with salt and pepper.
8. Pour the eggs into the skillet with the mushrooms and stir gently until the eggs are cooked and fluffy, about 5 minutes.
9. Serve hot, offering a hearty and healthy start to your day.

Nutritional Information: Kcal: 275, Cho: 2g, Fat: 21g, Na: 410mg, Pro: 19g

Grilled Chicken Sausage with Tomato Salsa

Servings: 2
Prep Time: 10 minutes
Cook Time: 10 minutes

Ingredients:

1. 2 chicken sausages (200g)
2. 2 medium tomatoes, diced (300g)
3. 1 small onion, finely chopped (70g)
4. 1 jalapeño, minced (14g)
5. 1/4 cup chopped fresh cilantro (4g)
6. Juice of 1 lime (30ml)
7. Salt and pepper to taste

Instructions:

8. Preheat grill to medium-high heat (350°F or 177°C).
9. Grill chicken sausages until fully cooked and browned, about 5 minutes per side.
10. In a bowl, combine diced tomatoes, chopped onion, minced jalapeño, cilantro, lime juice, salt, and pepper.
11. Stir the salsa well to mix.
12. Serve the grilled sausages topped with the fresh tomato salsa.

Nutritional Information: Kcal: 260, Cho: 10g, Fat: 15g, Na: 670mg, Pro: 20g

Tofu Scramble with Spinach and Peppers

Servings: 2
Prep Time: 5 minutes
Cook Time: 10 minutes

Ingredients:

1. 1 block firm tofu, drained and crumbled (400g)
2. 1 cup fresh spinach, chopped (30g)
3. 1 bell pepper, diced (150g)
4. 1 tablespoon olive oil (15ml)
5. 1 teaspoon turmeric (3g)
6. Salt and pepper to taste

Instructions:

7. Heat olive oil in a skillet over medium heat (350°F or 177°C).
8. Add the diced bell pepper to the skillet and sauté for 3 minutes.
9. Stir in the crumbled tofu and turmeric, cooking for another 5 minutes until the tofu is heated through.
10. Add the chopped spinach and cook until wilted, about 2 minutes.
11. Season with salt and pepper.
12. Serve hot, garnished with additional fresh herbs if desired.

Nutritional Information: Kcal: 220, Cho: 12g, Fat: 14g, Na: 120mg, Pro: 18g

Egg White Frittata with Asparagus

Servings: 2
Prep Time: 5 minutes
Cook Time: 20 minutes

Ingredients:

1. 6 egg whites (180ml)
2. 1 cup chopped asparagus (134g)
3. 1/2 cup diced onions (85g)
4. 1/4 cup low-fat milk (60ml)
5. 1 tablespoon olive oil (15ml)
6. Salt and pepper to taste

Instructions:

7. Preheat the oven to 375°F (190°C).
8. Heat olive oil in an oven-safe skillet over medium heat.

9. Sauté onions and asparagus until tender, about 5 minutes.

10. In a bowl, whisk together egg whites, milk, salt, and pepper.

11. Pour the egg mixture over the sautéed vegetables.

12. Transfer the skillet to the oven and bake until the eggs are set, about 15 minutes.

13. Serve warm, cut into wedges.

Nutritional Information: Kcal: 180, Cho: 8g, Fat: 10g, Na: 220mg, Pro: 15g

Baked Eggs in Avocado Cups

Servings: 2
Prep Time: 5 minutes
Cook Time: 15 minutes

Ingredients:

1. 2 avocados, halved and pitted (400g)
2. 4 eggs (200g)
3. Salt and pepper to taste
4. 2 tablespoons chopped chives (6g)

Instructions:

5. Preheat the oven to 425°F (220°C).
6. Scoop out a little more avocado from the pit area to enlarge the space.
7. Place the avocado halves in a baking dish to keep them stable.
8. Crack an egg into each avocado half, being careful not to spill the egg white.
9. Season with salt and pepper.
10. Bake in the preheated oven until the egg whites are set and yolks are cooked to your liking, about 15 minutes.
11. Garnish with chopped chives and serve immediately.

Nutritional Information: Kcal: 300, Cho: 9g, Fat: 25g, Na: 120mg, Pro: 13g

Oatmeal with Turmeric and Almonds

Servings: 2
Prep Time: 5 minutes
Cook Time: 10 minutes

Ingredients:

1. 1 cup rolled oats (90g)
2. 2 cups water (480ml)
3. 1/2 teaspoon turmeric (1g)
4. 1 tablespoon honey (21g)
5. 1/4 cup sliced almonds (30g)

Instructions:

6. Bring water to a boil in a medium saucepan (212°F or 100°C).
7. Add the rolled oats and turmeric, reducing heat to a simmer.
8. Cook for about 10 minutes, stirring occasionally until the oats are soft.
9. Remove from heat and stir in honey.
10. Serve topped with sliced almonds.

Nutritional Information: Kcal: 270, Cho: 45g, Fat: 7g, Na: 5mg, Pro: 8g

Quinoa Porridge with Mixed Berries

Servings: 2
Prep Time: 5 minutes
Cook Time: 15 minutes

Ingredients:

1. 1 cup quinoa (170g)
2. 2 cups almond milk (480ml)
3. 1 cup mixed berries, fresh or frozen (150g)
4. 2 tablespoons maple syrup (30ml)

Instructions:

5. Rinse quinoa under cold water.
6. In a pot, combine quinoa and almond milk, bringing to a boil (212°F or 100°C).

7. Reduce heat to low and simmer for 15 minutes, or until quinoa is fully cooked.
8. Stir in mixed berries and cook for an additional 2 minutes.
9. Drizzle with maple syrup before serving.

Nutritional Information: Kcal: 355, Cho: 65g, Fat: 8g, Na: 95mg, Pro: 9g

Buckwheat with Honey and Cinnamon

Servings: 2
Prep Time: 5 minutes
Cook Time: 10 minutes

Ingredients:
1. 1 cup buckwheat groats (170g)
2. 2 cups water (480ml)
3. 1/2 teaspoon cinnamon (1g)
4. 2 tablespoons honey (40g)

Instructions:
5. Bring water to a boil in a medium pot (212°F or 100°C).
6. Add buckwheat groats and cinnamon, then reduce heat to a simmer.
7. Cover and let simmer for about 10 minutes or until tender.
8. Stir in honey before serving.

Nutritional Information: Kcal: 320, Cho: 71g, Fat: 1g, Na: 10mg, Pro: 6g

Millet Porridge with Apple and Flaxseeds

Servings: 2
Prep Time: 5 minutes
Cook Time: 20 minutes

Ingredients:
1. 1 cup millet (200g)
2. 2 1/2 cups water (600ml)
3. 1 medium apple, diced (182g)
4. 2 tablespoons ground flaxseeds (14g)

Instructions:
5. Rinse millet under cold water.
6. In a saucepan, combine millet and water, and bring to a boil (212°F or 100°C).
7. Reduce to a simmer, cover, and cook for 15 minutes.
8. Add the diced apple and continue to cook for 5 more minutes.
9. Stir in ground flaxseeds before serving.

Nutritional Information: Kcal: 410, Cho: 77g, Fat: 7g, Na: 10mg, Pro: 11g

Barley Porridge with Dates and Cardamom

Servings: 2
Prep Time: 5 minutes
Cook Time: 25 minutes

Ingredients:

1. 1 cup pearled barley (200g)
2. 2 1/2 cups water (600ml)
3. 1/2 cup chopped dates (80g)
4. 1/2 teaspoon ground cardamom (1g)

Instructions:

5. Rinse barley under cold water.
6. In a saucepan, bring barley and water to a boil (212°F or 100°C).
7. Reduce heat and simmer for 20 minutes or until barley is tender.
8. Stir in chopped dates and cardamom, cooking for an additional 5 minutes.
9. Serve warm.

Nutritional Information: Kcal: 430, Cho: 91g, Fat: 1g, Na: 15mg, Pro: 10g

Amaranth Porridge with Cherry and Walnut

Servings: 2
Prep Time: 5 minutes
Cook Time: 20 minutes

Ingredients:

1. 1 cup amaranth (200g)
2. 2 1/2 cups water (600ml)
3. 1/2 cup cherries, pitted and halved (75g)
4. 1/4 cup chopped walnuts (30g)

Instructions:

5. Rinse amaranth under cold running water.
6. In a pot, bring amaranth and water to a boil (212°F or 100°C).
7. Reduce heat to a simmer, cover, and cook for 18 minutes, or until water is absorbed.
8. Remove from heat and stir in cherries and walnuts.
9. Serve warm, enjoying the nutty flavor and burst of cherry sweetness.

Nutritional Information: Kcal: 390, Cho: 67g, Fat: 11g, Na: 5mg, Pro: 11g

CHAPTER 7:
Lunch Recipes

SALADS: LOADED WITH ANTI-INFLAMMATORY INGREDIENTS

Quinoa and Roasted Vegetable Salad

Servings: 2
Prep Time: 5 minutes
Cook Time: 20 minutes

Ingredients:

1. 1/2 cup quinoa (85g)
2. 1 cup water (240ml)
3. 1 small zucchini, chopped (120g)
4. 1 red bell pepper, chopped (150g)
5. 1/2 red onion, sliced (60g)
6. 2 tablespoons olive oil (30ml)
7. Salt and pepper to taste

Instructions:

8. Preheat oven to 400°F (204°C).
9. Toss zucchini, bell pepper, and onion with one tablespoon olive oil, salt, and pepper. Spread on a baking sheet and roast for 20 minutes, stirring halfway through.
10. Meanwhile, rinse quinoa under cold water. Bring water and quinoa to a boil in a saucepan. Reduce to a simmer, cover, and cook until all water is absorbed, about 15 minutes.
11. Combine roasted vegetables with quinoa, drizzle with remaining olive oil, and serve warm.

Nutritional Information: Kcal: 320, Cho: 45g, Fat: 14g, Na: 30mg, Pro: 8g

Spinach and Walnut Salad with Citrus Vinaigrette

Servings: 2
Prep Time: 10 minutes
Cook Time: 0 minutes

Ingredients:

1. 4 cups baby spinach (120g)
2. 1/4 cup chopped walnuts (30g)
3. 2 oranges, peeled and sections cut (280g)
4. 2 tablespoons olive oil (30ml)
5. 1 tablespoon lemon juice (15ml)
6. Salt and pepper to taste

Instructions:

7. Place spinach, orange sections, and walnuts in a large salad bowl.
8. In a small bowl, whisk together olive oil, lemon juice, salt, and pepper to make the vinaigrette.
9. Pour the vinaigrette over the salad and toss gently to combine.
10. Serve immediately, offering a refreshing and nourishing meal.

Nutritional Information: Kcal: 315, Cho: 27g, Fat: 23g, Na: 45mg, Pro: 5g

Broccoli, Chickpea, and Avocado Salad

Servings: 2
Prep Time: 10 minutes
Cook Time: 0 minutes

Ingredients:

1. 2 cups broccoli florets (150g)
2. 1 cup canned chickpeas, rinsed and drained (164g)
3. 1 avocado, diced (200g)
4. 2 tablespoons lemon juice (30ml)
5. 2 tablespoons olive oil (30ml)
6. Salt and pepper to taste

Instructions:

7. Steam broccoli florets until just tender, about 5 minutes.
8. In a salad bowl, combine steamed broccoli, chickpeas, and diced avocado.
9. Whisk together lemon juice, olive oil, salt, and pepper.

10. Drizzle the dressing over the salad and toss well to coat.
11. Serve chilled for a crunchy and creamy texture.

Nutritional Information: Kcal: 400, Cho: 35g, Fat: 27g, Na: 300mg, Pro: 10g

Kale, Carrot, and Almond Salad

Servings: 2
Prep Time: 10 minutes
Cook Time: 0 minutes

Ingredients:

1. 3 cups chopped kale (90g)
2. 1 large carrot, shredded (120g)
3. 1/4 cup sliced almonds (30g)
4. 2 tablespoons olive oil (30ml)
5. 1 tablespoon apple cider vinegar (15ml)
6. Salt and pepper to taste

Instructions:

7. In a large bowl, combine kale, shredded carrot, and sliced almonds.
8. In a small bowl, whisk together olive oil, apple cider vinegar, salt, and pepper.
9. Pour the dressing over the kale mixture and toss to coat evenly.
10. Massage the kale gently with your hands to soften the leaves.
11. Serve fresh for a crunchy and tangy salad experience.

Nutritional Information: Kcal: 295, Cho: 18g, Fat: 23g, Na: 75mg, Pro: 7g

Beetroot and Goat Cheese Salad

Servings: 2
Prep Time: 10 minutes
Cook Time: 0 minutes

Ingredients:

1. 2 medium beetroots, cooked and sliced (300g)
2. 1/4 cup crumbled goat cheese (30g)
3. 1/4 cup chopped walnuts (30g)
4. 2 tablespoons olive oil (30ml)
5. 1 tablespoon balsamic vinegar (15ml)
6. Salt and pepper to taste

Instructions:

7. Arrange sliced beetroots on a plate.
8. Sprinkle crumbled goat cheese and chopped walnuts over the beetroots.
9. In a small bowl, whisk together olive oil, balsamic vinegar, salt, and pepper.
10. Drizzle the dressing over the salad.

11. Serve immediately, enjoying the sweet and earthy flavors balanced by the tangy goat cheese.

Nutritional Information: Kcal: 370, Cho: 20g, Fat: 29g, Na: 215mg, Pro: 9g

Arugula, Fennel, and Orange Salad

Servings: 2
Prep Time: 10 minutes
Cook Time: 0 minutes

Ingredients:

1. 3 cups arugula (90g)
2. 1 small fennel bulb, thinly sliced (130g)
3. 2 oranges, peeled and sections cut (280g)
4. 2 tablespoons olive oil (30ml)
5. 1 tablespoon lemon juice (15ml)
6. Salt and pepper to taste

Instructions:

7. In a salad bowl, combine arugula and thinly sliced fennel.
8. Add orange sections to the bowl.
9. In a small bowl, whisk together olive oil, lemon juice, salt, and pepper.
10. Drizzle the dressing over the salad and toss gently to coat.
11. Serve immediately, enjoying the crisp freshness of fennel with the sweet citrus burst from oranges.

Nutritional Information: Kcal: 185, Cho: 21g, Fat: 11g, Na: 45mg, Pro: 3g

Lentil Salad with Cucumber and Mint

Servings: 2
Prep Time: 15 minutes
Cook Time: 20 minutes

Ingredients:

1. 1 cup dried lentils (200g)
2. 1 large cucumber, diced (240g)
3. 1/4 cup fresh mint leaves, chopped (6g)
4. 2 tablespoons olive oil (30ml)
5. 1 tablespoon red wine vinegar (15ml)
6. Salt and pepper to taste

Instructions:

7. Rinse lentils and bring to a boil in a pot with sufficient water. Reduce heat and simmer until tender, about 20 minutes.
8. Drain lentils and allow to cool.
9. In a large bowl, combine cooled lentils, diced cucumber, and chopped mint.

10. Whisk together olive oil, red wine vinegar, salt, and pepper in a small bowl.

11. Pour the dressing over the lentil mixture and toss to combine thoroughly.

12. Serve chilled or at room temperature for a refreshing and nutritious meal.

Nutritional Information: Kcal: 340, Cho: 38g, Fat: 14g, Na: 30mg, Pro: 18g

Cabbage and Hemp Seed Salad

Servings: 2
Prep Time: 10 minutes
Cook Time: 0 minutes

Ingredients:

1. 2 cups shredded cabbage (150g)
2. 1/4 cup hemp seeds (30g)
3. 2 carrots, shredded (120g)
4. 2 tablespoons apple cider vinegar (30ml)
5. 1 tablespoon honey (21g)
6. 1 tablespoon olive oil (15ml)
7. Salt and pepper to taste

Instructions:

8. In a large salad bowl, combine shredded cabbage, shredded carrots, and hemp seeds.

9. In a small bowl, whisk together apple cider vinegar, honey, olive oil, salt, and pepper to create the dressing.

10. Pour the dressing over the cabbage mixture and toss well to ensure all ingredients are evenly coated.

11. Let the salad sit for about 5 minutes before serving to allow flavors to meld.

12. Serve as a crunchy, nutritious side dish or a light main course.

Nutritional Information: Kcal: 245, Cho: 20g, Fat: 15g, Na: 55mg, Pro: 7g

Carrot and Ginger Soup

Servings: 2
Prep Time: 10 minutes
Cook Time: 20 minutes

Ingredients:
1. 4 carrots, peeled and chopped (400g)
2. 2 inches fresh ginger, peeled and minced (30g)
3. 1 onion, chopped (110g)
4. 2 cups vegetable broth (480ml)
5. 1 tablespoon olive oil (15ml)
6. Salt and pepper to taste

Instructions:
7. Heat olive oil in a large pot over medium heat (350°F or 177°C).
8. Add chopped onion and minced ginger, sauté until onion is translucent, about 5 minutes.
9. Add chopped carrots and cook for another 5 minutes.
10. Pour in vegetable broth, bring to a boil, then reduce to a simmer and cover. Cook until carrots are tender, about 10 minutes.
11. Blend the soup in a blender or use an immersion blender until smooth.
12. Season with salt and pepper to taste and serve hot.

Nutritional Information: Kcal: 180, Cho: 27g, Fat: 7g, Na: 580mg, Pro: 2g

Tomato Basil Soup

Servings: 2
Prep Time: 5 minutes
Cook Time: 20 minutes

Ingredients:
1. 4 tomatoes, chopped (400g)
2. 1 onion, diced (110g)
3. 2 garlic cloves, minced (6g)

4. 1/4 cup fresh basil, chopped (6g)
5. 2 cups vegetable broth (480ml)
6. 1 tablespoon olive oil (15ml)
7. Salt and pepper to taste

Instructions:

8. Heat olive oil in a pot over medium heat (350°F or 177°C).
9. Add onion and garlic, sauté until onion is soft, about 5 minutes.
10. Stir in chopped tomatoes and cook for another 5 minutes.
11. Add vegetable broth and bring to a boil. Reduce heat to low, simmer for 10 minutes.
12. Add chopped basil, then blend the soup until smooth.
13. Season with salt and pepper, serve warm.

Nutritional Information: Kcal: 140, Cho: 18g, Fat: 7g, Na: 480mg, Pro: 3g

Lentil and Spinach Soup

Servings: 2
Prep Time: 10 minutes
Cook Time: 25 minutes

Ingredients:

1. 1 cup dried lentils, rinsed (200g)
2. 2 cups spinach, chopped (60g)
3. 1 carrot, diced (100g)
4. 1 onion, chopped (110g)
5. 2 cloves garlic, minced (6g)
6. 4 cups vegetable broth (960ml)
7. 1 tablespoon olive oil (15ml)
8. Salt and pepper to taste

Instructions:

9. Heat olive oil in a large pot over medium heat (350°F or 177°C).
10. Add onion and garlic, sauté until onion is translucent.
11. Add carrots and lentils, stir to combine.
12. Pour in vegetable broth and bring to a boil. Reduce to a simmer and cook until lentils are tender, about 20 minutes.
13. Stir in chopped spinach and cook until wilted, about 2 minutes.
14. Season with salt and pepper, serve hot.

Nutritional Information: Kcal: 315, Cho: 45g, Fat: 7g, Na: 590mg, Pro: 18g

Chicken and Vegetable Broth

Servings: 2
Prep Time: 10 minutes
Cook Time: 30 minutes

Ingredients:

1. 2 chicken breasts (500g)
2. 4 cups water (960ml)
3. 1 onion, quartered (110g)
4. 2 carrots, chopped (200g)
5. 2 celery stalks, chopped (80g)
6. 2 garlic cloves (6g)
7. Salt and pepper to taste

Instructions:

8. In a large pot, combine chicken, water, onion, carrots, celery, and garlic. Season with salt and pepper.
9. Bring to a boil over high heat (212°F or 100°C), then reduce to a simmer.
10. Cover and let simmer for 30 minutes, or until chicken is cooked through.
11. Remove chicken, shred it, and return to the pot.
12. Adjust seasoning if necessary, and serve hot.

Nutritional Information: Kcal: 255, Cho: 8g, Fat: 5g, Na: 110mg, Pro: 42g

Butternut Squash Soup

Servings: 2
Prep Time: 10 minutes
Cook Time: 25 minutes

Ingredients:

1. 2 cups butternut squash, cubed (300g)
2. 1 onion, diced (110g)
3. 2 cups vegetable broth (480ml)
4. 1/2 cup light coconut milk (120ml)
5. 1 tablespoon olive oil (15ml)
6. Salt and pepper to taste
7. 1 teaspoon ground cinnamon (2g)

Instructions:

8. Heat olive oil in a large pot over medium heat (350°F or 177°C).
9. Add diced onion, sauté until soft, about 5 minutes.
10. Add butternut squash and cook for another 5 minutes.
11. Pour in vegetable broth, bring to a boil, then reduce to a simmer.
12. Cook until squash is tender, about 15 minutes.

13. Stir in coconut milk and cinnamon.
14. Blend the soup until smooth. Season with salt and pepper, and serve warm.

Nutritional Information: Kcal: 235, Cho: 37g, Fat: 8g, Na: 480mg, Pro: 3g

Mushroom and Thyme Soup

Servings: 2
Prep Time: 10 minutes
Cook Time: 20 minutes

Ingredients:

1. 2 cups sliced mushrooms (150g)
2. 1 onion, finely chopped (110g)
3. 2 cloves garlic, minced (6g)
4. 4 cups vegetable broth (960ml)
5. 1 tablespoon fresh thyme leaves (3g)
6. 1 tablespoon olive oil (15ml)
7. Salt and pepper to taste

Instructions:

8. Heat olive oil in a large pot over medium heat (350°F or 177°C).
9. Add onion and garlic, sauté until soft, about 5 minutes.
10. Add mushrooms and thyme, cook until mushrooms are browned, about 10 minutes.
11. Pour in vegetable broth and bring to a simmer.
12. Cook for an additional 10 minutes.
13. Blend half of the soup to create a creamy texture, then recombine.
14. Season with salt and pepper to taste, and serve warm.

Nutritional Information: Kcal: 130, Cho: 18g, Fat: 5g, Na: 960mg, Pro: 4g

Pea and Mint Soup

Servings: 2
Prep Time: 5 minutes
Cook Time: 15 minutes

Ingredients:

1. 2 cups frozen peas (300g)
2. 1/4 cup fresh mint leaves (6g)
3. 1 onion, chopped (110g)
4. 3 cups vegetable broth (720ml)

5. 1 tablespoon olive oil (15ml)
6. Salt and pepper to taste

Instructions:

7. Heat olive oil in a pot over medium heat (350°F or 177°C).
8. Add chopped onion, sauté until translucent, about 5 minutes.
9. Add peas and vegetable broth, bring to a boil.
10. Reduce heat and simmer for 10 minutes.
11. Stir in fresh mint leaves.
12. Blend the soup until smooth.
13. Season with salt and pepper, serve hot.

Nutritional Information: Kcal: 220, Cho: 34g, Fat: 7g, Na: 890mg, Pro: 8g

Spicy Pumpkin Soup

Servings: 2
Prep Time: 10 minutes
Cook Time: 20 minutes

Ingredients:

1. 2 cups pumpkin puree (450g)
2. 1 small red chili, finely chopped (15g)
3. 1 onion, chopped (110g)
4. 3 cups vegetable broth (720ml)
5. 1 teaspoon ground cumin (2g)
6. 1 tablespoon olive oil (15ml)
7. Salt and pepper to taste

Instructions:

8. Heat olive oil in a pot over medium heat (350°F or 177°C).
9. Add chopped onion and chili, sauté until onion is soft, about 5 minutes.
10. Stir in pumpkin puree, cumin, and vegetable broth.
11. Bring to a boil, then reduce heat and simmer for 15 minutes.
12. Blend the soup until smooth.
13. Season with salt and pepper, serve hot with a dollop of yogurt if desired for cooling.

Nutritional Information: Kcal: 180, Cho: 28g, Fat: 7g, Na: 760mg, Pro: 3g

Grilled Chicken with Quinoa and Steamed Vegetables

Servings: 2
Prep Time: 10 minutes
Cook Time: 20 minutes

Ingredients:

1. 2 chicken breasts, boneless and skinless (400g)
2. 1/2 cup quinoa (85g)
3. 1 cup water (240ml)
4. 1 cup broccoli florets (150g)
5. 1 carrot, sliced (60g)
6. 2 tablespoons olive oil (30ml)
7. Salt and pepper to taste

Instructions:

8. Preheat grill to medium-high heat (375°F or 190°C).
9. Brush chicken breasts with 1 tablespoon olive oil and season with salt and pepper.
10. Grill chicken for about 10 minutes on each side or until fully cooked.
11. Meanwhile, rinse quinoa under cold water, bring water and quinoa to a boil in a saucepan, reduce to a simmer, cover, and cook until water is absorbed, about 15 minutes.
12. Steam broccoli and carrots until tender, about 7 minutes.
13. Serve grilled chicken on a bed of quinoa with steamed vegetables on the side.

Nutritional Information: Kcal: 560, Cho: 39g, Fat: 23g, Na: 220mg, Pro: 48g

Baked Salmon with Asparagus and Sweet Potatoes

Servings: 2
Prep Time: 10 minutes
Cook Time: 25 minutes

Ingredients:

1. 2 salmon fillets (400g)
2. 1 large sweet potato, sliced into rounds (200g)

3. 1 bunch asparagus, trimmed (200g)
4. 2 tablespoons olive oil (30ml)
5. Salt and pepper to taste

Instructions:

6. Preheat oven to 400°F (204°C).
7. Arrange sweet potato rounds and asparagus on a baking sheet, drizzle with 1 tablespoon olive oil, and season with salt and pepper.
8. Place salmon fillets on the same sheet, brush with remaining olive oil, and season.
9. Bake in the preheated oven for 20-25 minutes or until salmon is cooked through and vegetables are tender.
10. Serve immediately, enjoying a harmonious blend of flavors.

Nutritional Information: Kcal: 520, Cho: 23g, Fat: 29g, Na: 180mg, Pro: 45g

Stir-Fried Tofu with Broccoli and Bell Peppers

Servings: 2
Prep Time: 10 minutes
Cook Time: 10 minutes

Ingredients:

1. 1 block firm tofu, drained and cubed (300g)
2. 1 cup broccoli florets (150g)
3. 1 red bell pepper, sliced (150g)
4. 2 tablespoons soy sauce (30ml)
5. 1 tablespoon sesame oil (15ml)
6. 1 garlic clove, minced (3g)

Instructions:

7. Heat sesame oil in a large skillet over medium-high heat (350°F or 177°C).
8. Add garlic, tofu, and soy sauce, stir-fry for 5 minutes.
9. Add broccoli and bell pepper, continue to stir-fry until vegetables are just tender, about 5 more minutes.
10. Serve hot, garnished with sesame seeds if desired.

Nutritional Information: Kcal: 340, Cho: 15g, Fat: 22g, Na: 660mg, Pro: 22g

Beef Stew with Root Vegetables

Servings: 2
Prep Time: 15 minutes
Cook Time: 1 hour 30 minutes

Ingredients:

1. 1/2 pound beef stew meat, cut into chunks (225g)
2. 2 carrots, peeled and chopped (120g)

3. 2 parsnips, peeled and chopped (120g)
4. 1 onion, chopped (110g)
5. 4 cups beef broth (960ml)
6. 1 tablespoon olive oil (15ml)
7. Salt and pepper to taste

Instructions:

8. Heat olive oil in a large pot over medium heat (350°F or 177°C).
9. Brown beef chunks on all sides.
10. Add onions, carrots, and parsnips, sauté for a few minutes.
11. Pour in beef broth, bring to a boil, then reduce to a simmer.
12. Cover and let simmer for about 1.5 hours or until the meat is tender.
13. Season with salt and pepper, serve hot.

Nutritional Information: Kcal: 460, Cho: 22g, Fat: 25g, Na: 890mg, Pro: 36g

Shrimp and Avocado Wrap

Servings: 2
Prep Time: 10 minutes
Cook Time: 5 minutes

Ingredients:

1. 12 large shrimp, peeled and deveined (180g)
2. 2 whole wheat wraps (90g)
3. 1 avocado, sliced (200g)
4. 1/4 cup Greek yogurt (60g)
5. 1 tablespoon lime juice (15ml)
6. 1/2 cup lettuce, shredded (35g)
7. Salt and pepper to taste

Instructions:

8. Heat a skillet over medium heat (350°F or 177°C) and cook shrimp until pink and opaque, about 2-3 minutes per side.
9. Spread Greek yogurt on each wrap.
10. Lay down lettuce, avocado slices, and cooked shrimp on the wraps.
11. Drizzle with lime juice and season with salt and pepper.
12. Roll up the wraps tightly and cut in half.
13. Serve immediately for a refreshing and satisfying meal.

Nutritional Information: Kcal: 420, Cho: 36g, Fat: 21g, Na: 480mg, Pro: 25g

Portobello Mushroom Steak

Servings: 2
Prep Time: 10 minutes
Cook Time: 15 minutes

Ingredients:

1. 4 large Portobello mushrooms, stems removed (480g)
2. 2 tablespoons balsamic vinegar (30ml)
3. 1 tablespoon olive oil (15ml)
4. 2 garlic cloves, minced (6g)
5. Salt and pepper to taste

Instructions:

6. Preheat grill to medium-high heat (375°F or 190°C).
7. In a small bowl, whisk together balsamic vinegar, olive oil, minced garlic, salt, and pepper.
8. Brush the mixture generously on both sides of the Portobello mushrooms.
9. Place mushrooms on the grill, gill side down, and cook for about 7-8 minutes on each side or until tender and grill marks appear.
10. Serve the grilled mushrooms as you would a steak.

Nutritional Information: Kcal: 130, Cho: 13g, Fat: 8g, Na: 10mg, Pro: 4g

Baked Trout with Lemon and Dill

Servings: 2
Prep Time: 5 minutes
Cook Time: 15 minutes

Ingredients:

1. 2 trout fillets (350g)
2. 1 lemon, thinly sliced (58g)
3. 2 tablespoons fresh dill, chopped (6g)
4. 1 tablespoon olive oil (15ml)
5. Salt and pepper to taste

Instructions:

6. Preheat oven to 400°F (204°C).
7. Line a baking sheet with foil and brush with olive oil.
8. Place trout fillets on the prepared sheet and season with salt and pepper.
9. Top each fillet with lemon slices and sprinkle with dill.
10. Bake in the preheated oven for about 12-15 minutes or until the trout is flaky and cooked through.
11. Serve hot, garnished with additional dill if desired.

Nutritional Information: Kcal: 290, Cho: 1g, Fat: 15g, Na: 75mg, Pro: 35g

Veggie and Quinoa Stuffed Peppers

Servings: 2
Prep Time: 15 minutes
Cook Time: 30 minutes

Ingredients:

1. 2 large bell peppers, halved and seeded (300g)
2. 1/2 cup cooked quinoa (85g)
3. 1/2 cup black beans, rinsed and drained (90g)
4. 1/2 cup corn kernels (80g)
5. 1/4 cup diced tomatoes (60g)
6. 1/4 cup chopped onions (40g)
7. 1 clove garlic, minced (3g)
8. 1/2 teaspoon cumin (1g)
9. 1 tablespoon olive oil (15ml)
10. Salt and pepper to taste

Instructions:

11. Preheat oven to 375°F (190°C).
12. Heat olive oil in a skillet over medium heat. Add onions and garlic, sauté until soft.
13. Stir in tomatoes, black beans, corn, and cumin. Cook for another 5 minutes.
14. Remove from heat, stir in cooked quinoa, and season with salt and pepper.
15. Spoon the quinoa and vegetable mixture into each bell pepper half.
16. Place stuffed peppers in a baking dish and cover with foil.
17. Bake for 25-30 minutes or until peppers are tender.
18. Serve hot, topped with fresh cilantro if desired.

Nutritional Information: Kcal: 290, Cho: 40g, Fat: 10g, Na: 200mg, Pro: 9g

CHAPTER 8:
Snack Recipes

ENERGY BOOSTERS: QUICK NUTRITIOUS OPTIONS

Almond and Date Energy Balls

Servings: 2
Prep Time: 15 minutes
Cook Time: 0 minutes

Ingredients:
1. 1 cup dates, pitted (200g)
2. 1/2 cup almonds (60g)
3. 1 tablespoon chia seeds (10g)
4. 1/2 teaspoon vanilla extract (2ml)

Instructions:
5. Place the pitted dates, almonds, chia seeds, and vanilla extract in a food processor.
6. Pulse until the mixture is well combined and sticks together when pressed.
7. Roll the mixture into small balls, about the size of a walnut.
8. Place the energy balls on a baking sheet lined with parchment paper and refrigerate for at least 1 hour to set.
9. Serve chilled as a quick and nutritious snack.

Nutritional Information: Kcal: 315, Cho: 53g, Fat: 11g, Na: 5mg, Pro: 7g

Pumpkin Seeds and Dried Cranberries

Servings: 2
Prep Time: 5 minutes
Cook Time: 0 minutes

Ingredients:

1. 1/4 cup pumpkin seeds (30g)
2. 1/4 cup dried cranberries (40g)

Instructions:

3. Mix pumpkin seeds and dried cranberries in a small bowl.
4. Divide the mixture into two portions.
5. Pack each portion into small containers or snack bags for an easy, on-the-go snack.

Nutritional Information: Kcal: 180, Cho: 20g, Fat: 9g, Na: 5mg, Pro: 5g

Cottage Cheese with Sliced Peaches

Servings: 2
Prep Time: 5 minutes
Cook Time: 0 minutes

Ingredients:

1. 1 cup cottage cheese, low-fat (225g)
2. 1 peach, sliced (150g)

Instructions:

3. Divide the cottage cheese between two bowls.
4. Top each bowl with sliced peaches.
5. Serve immediately for a refreshing and healthy snack or dessert.

Nutritional Information: Kcal: 150, Cho: 15g, Fat: 2g, Na: 400mg, Pro: 14g

Hard-Boiled Eggs with Spinach Dip

Servings: 2
Prep Time: 10 minutes
Cook Time: 10 minutes

Ingredients:

1. 4 eggs (200g)
2. 1 cup spinach, cooked and chopped (180g)
3. 1/4 cup Greek yogurt, non-fat (60g)
4. Salt and pepper to taste

Instructions:

5. Place eggs in a saucepan and cover with water. Bring to a boil over high heat (212°F or 100°C), then remove from heat, cover, and let sit for 10 minutes.
6. Cool the eggs under cold running water, peel them.
7. In a small bowl, mix the chopped spinach with Greek yogurt, salt, and pepper to create the dip.
8. Cut eggs in half and serve with the spinach dip.

Nutritional Information: Kcal: 235, Cho: 4g, Fat: 15g, Na: 310mg, Pro: 20g

Sweet Potato and Beet Chips

Servings: 2
Prep Time: 10 minutes
Cook Time: 25 minutes

Ingredients:

1. 1 medium sweet potato, thinly sliced (200g)
2. 1 medium beet, thinly sliced (175g)
3. 1 tablespoon olive oil (15ml)
4. Salt to taste

Instructions:

5. Preheat oven to 375°F (190°C).
6. Toss sweet potato and beet slices in olive oil and spread them in a single layer on a baking sheet lined with parchment paper.
7. Sprinkle lightly with salt.
8. Bake for 20-25 minutes, turning halfway through, until crisp and lightly browned.
9. Let cool before serving to enhance crispiness.

Nutritional Information: Kcal: 180, Cho: 23g, Fat: 9g, Na: 170mg, Pro: 2g

Walnut and Fig Bars

Servings: 2
Prep Time: 15 minutes
Cook Time: 0 minutes

Ingredients:

1. 1/2 cup dried figs, stems removed (75g)
2. 1/4 cup walnuts (30g)
3. 1/4 cup rolled oats (20g)
4. 1 tablespoon honey (15ml)

Instructions:

5. Place figs, walnuts, rolled oats, and honey in a food processor.
6. Pulse until the mixture is well combined and sticks together.
7. Line a small baking dish with parchment paper.
8. Press the mixture firmly into the dish.
9. Refrigerate for at least 1 hour to set.
10. Cut into bars and serve chilled for a nourishing snack.

Nutritional Information: Kcal: 295, Cho: 44g, Fat: 13g, Na: 5mg, Pro: 5g

Protein-Packed Trail Mix

Servings: 2
Prep Time: 5 minutes
Cook Time: 0 minutes

Ingredients:

1. 1/4 cup almonds (30g)
2. 1/4 cup pumpkin seeds (30g)
3. 1/4 cup dried cranberries (40g)
4. 2 tablespoons sunflower seeds (18g)

Instructions:

5. Combine almonds, pumpkin seeds, dried cranberries, and sunflower seeds in a bowl.
6. Mix well to ensure even distribution.
7. Divide the mixture into two portions.
8. Pack in airtight containers or snack bags for a convenient on-the-go energy boost.

Nutritional Information: Kcal: 260, Cho: 20g, Fat: 18g, Na: 5mg, Pro: 8g

Celery Sticks with Almond Butter

Servings: 2
Prep Time: 5 minutes
Cook Time: 0 minutes

Ingredients:
1. 4 celery stalks, cut into sticks (120g)
2. 2 tablespoons almond butter (32g)

Instructions:
3. Wash and dry the celery stalks thoroughly.
4. Cut the celery into stick-sized pieces.
5. Spread almond butter evenly over each celery stick.
6. Arrange the celery sticks on a plate and serve as a crunchy, nutritious snack.

Nutritional Information: Kcal: 160, Cho: 8g, Fat: 12g, Na: 80mg, Pro: 5g

Cucumber and Hummus

Servings: 2
Prep Time: 5 minutes
Cook Time: 0 minutes

Ingredients:
1. 1 large cucumber, sliced (250g)
2. 1/4 cup hummus (60g)

Instructions:
3. Rinse the cucumber and slice into thin rounds.
4. Spoon hummus into a small serving bowl.
5. Arrange cucumber slices around the bowl for dipping.
6. Serve immediately for a refreshing and filling snack.

Nutritional Information: Kcal: 105, Cho: 12g, Fat: 5g, Na: 200mg, Pro: 4g

Sliced Apples with Peanut Butter

Servings: 2
Prep Time: 5 minutes
Cook Time: 0 minutes

1. 2 medium apples, sliced (360g)
2. 2 tablespoons peanut butter (32g)

Instructions:

3. Core and slice the apples into thin wedges.
4. Place peanut butter in a small bowl.
5. Dip apple slices into peanut butter to enjoy a sweet and creamy snack.

Nutritional Information: Kcal: 280, Cho: 34g, Fat: 16g, Na: 150mg, Pro: 6g

Mixed Berry Salad

Servings: 2
Prep Time: 5 minutes
Cook Time: 0 minutes

Ingredients:

1. 1 cup strawberries, halved (152g)
2. 1 cup blueberries (148g)
3. 1 cup raspberries (123g)
4. 1 tablespoon honey (21g)

Instructions:

5. Combine strawberries, blueberries, and raspberries in a large bowl.
6. Drizzle honey over the berries and gently toss to coat.
7. Chill in the refrigerator for a few minutes before serving.

Nutritional Information: Kcal: 140, Cho: 34g, Fat: 1g, Na: 2mg, Pro: 2g

Roasted Chickpeas with Sea Salt

Servings: 2
Prep Time: 5 minutes
Cook Time: 30 minutes

Ingredients:
1. 1 cup chickpeas, drained and dried (164g)
2. 1 tablespoon olive oil (15ml)
3. 1/2 teaspoon sea salt (3g)

Instructions:
4. Preheat oven to 400°F (204°C).
5. Toss chickpeas with olive oil and spread on a baking sheet.
6. Roast in the oven for 25-30 minutes or until crispy.
7. Sprinkle with sea salt immediately after removing from the oven.
8. Let cool before serving as a crunchy, savory snack.

Nutritional Information: Kcal: 215, Cho: 27g, Fat: 9g, Na: 300mg, Pro: 7g

Bell Pepper Strips with Guacamole

Servings: 2
Prep Time: 10 minutes
Cook Time: 0 minutes

Ingredients:
1. 2 bell peppers, assorted colors, sliced into strips (300g)
2. 1 ripe avocado, mashed (200g)
3. 1 small tomato, diced (100g)
4. 1 tablespoon lime juice (15ml)
5. 1/4 teaspoon salt (1g)
6. 1 tablespoon chopped cilantro (1g)

Instructions:
7. In a medium bowl, combine the mashed avocado, diced tomato, lime juice, salt, and chopped cilantro.
8. Stir well to create a smooth guacamole.
9. Arrange bell pepper strips on a plate.
10. Serve the guacamole alongside the bell pepper strips for dipping.

Nutritional Information: Kcal: 200, Cho: 20g, Fat: 13g, Na: 300mg, Pro: 4g

Zucchini and Carrot Fritters

Servings: 2
Prep Time: 10 minutes
Cook Time: 10 minutes

Ingredients:

1. 1 medium zucchini, grated (200g)
2. 1 large carrot, grated (120g)
3. 1 egg, beaten (50g)
4. 2 tablespoons whole wheat flour (16g)
5. 1/4 teaspoon salt (1g)
6. 1/4 teaspoon black pepper (1g)
7. 2 tablespoons olive oil (30ml)

Instructions:

8. Squeeze excess moisture from the grated zucchini and carrot using a clean cloth.
9. In a bowl, mix the zucchini, carrot, beaten egg, flour, salt, and pepper.
10. Heat olive oil in a non-stick skillet over medium heat (350°F or 177°C).
11. Scoop spoonfuls of the mixture into the skillet, flattening into fritters.
12. Cook for about 5 minutes per side until golden brown and cooked through.
13. Serve hot.

Nutritional Information: Kcal: 240, Cho: 18g, Fat: 17g, Na: 300mg, Pro: 7g

Spiced Edamame Pods

Servings: 2
Prep Time: 5 minutes
Cook Time: 5 minutes

Ingredients:

1. 2 cups edamame pods, fresh or frozen (300g)
2. 1 tablespoon olive oil (15ml)
3. 1/2 teaspoon chili powder (1g)
4. 1/4 teaspoon garlic powder (0.5g)
5. 1/4 teaspoon salt (1g)

Instructions:

6. Heat olive oil in a large skillet over medium heat (350°F or 177°C).
7. Add the edamame pods to the skillet.
8. Sprinkle with chili powder, garlic powder, and salt.
9. Sauté for about 5 minutes, stirring frequently until the edamame is heated through and coated with spices.
10. Serve warm for a tasty and nutritious snack.

Nutritional Information: Kcal: 190, Cho: 13g, Fat: 11g, Na: 300mg, Pro: 12g

Green Detox Smoothie

Servings: 2
Prep Time: 5 minutes
Cook Time: 0 minutes

Ingredients:

1. 1 cup spinach leaves (30g)
2. 1 small cucumber, chopped (150g)
3. 1 green apple, cored and sliced (180g)
4. Juice of 1 lemon (30ml)
5. 1 inch ginger, peeled (15g)
6. 1 cup water (240ml)

Instructions:

7. Place spinach, cucumber, apple, lemon juice, ginger, and water in a blender.
8. Blend on high until smooth and fully combined.
9. Pour into glasses and serve immediately for a refreshing and cleansing boost.

Nutritional Information: Kcal: 95, Cho: 23g, Fat: 0.5g, Na: 20mg, Pro: 1g

Carrot and Beet Juice

Servings: 2
Prep Time: 10 minutes
Cook Time: 0 minutes

Ingredients:

1. 3 carrots, peeled (180g)
2. 1 large beet, peeled and quartered (175g)
3. 1/2 lemon, juiced (15ml)

Instructions:

4. Run carrots and beet through a juicer.
5. Stir in the lemon juice.
6. Serve immediately, enjoy this earthy and vibrant juice full of vitamins.

Nutritional Information: Kcal: 90, Cho: 21g, Fat: 0.5g, Na: 85mg, Pro: 2g

Pineapple and Mint Juice

Servings: 2
Prep Time: 5 minutes
Cook Time: 0 minutes

Ingredients:

1. 2 cups pineapple chunks (330g)
2. 1/4 cup fresh mint leaves (6g)
3. 1 cup water (240ml)

Instructions:

4. Place pineapple chunks, mint leaves, and water in a blender.
5. Blend until smooth.
6. Strain through a mesh sieve if desired and serve chilled.

Nutritional Information: Kcal: 100, Cho: 25g, Fat: 0.5g, Na: 2mg, Pro: 1g

Berry and Yogurt Smoothie

Servings: 2
Prep Time: 5 minutes
Cook Time: 0 minutes

Ingredients:

1. 1 cup mixed berries (strawberries, blueberries, raspberries) (150g)
2. 1 cup Greek yogurt, non-fat (245g)
3. 1 tablespoon honey (15ml)

Instructions:

4. Combine berries, yogurt, and honey in a blender.
5. Blend until smooth.
6. Serve immediately for a creamy and delicious smoothie packed with antioxidants.

Nutritional Information: Kcal: 150, Cho: 28g, Fat: 0.5g, Na: 50mg, Pro: 10g

Pomegranate and Lime Juice

Servings: 2
Prep Time: 5 minutes
Cook Time: 0 minutes

Ingredients:

1. Seeds from 1 pomegranate (175g)
2. Juice of 1 lime (15ml)
3. 1 cup water (240ml)

Instructions:

4. Place pomegranate seeds, lime juice, and water in a blender.
5. Blend until smooth.
6. Strain the mixture to remove any seeds and serve chilled.

Nutritional Information: Kcal: 85, Cho: 19g, Fat: 1g, Na: 5mg, Pro: 1g

Aloe Vera and Cucumber Juice

Servings: 2
Prep Time: 10 minutes
Cook Time: 0 minutes

Ingredients:

1. 1/2 cup aloe vera gel (freshly scooped) (120g)
2. 1 large cucumber, peeled and chopped (250g)
3. 1 tablespoon lemon juice (15ml)
4. 1 cup water (240ml)

Instructions:

5. Combine aloe vera gel, chopped cucumber, lemon juice, and water in a blender.
6. Blend on high until the mixture is completely smooth.
7. Strain the juice through a fine mesh sieve to remove any pulp.
8. Serve chilled for a refreshing and hydrating drink.

Nutritional Information: Kcal: 35, Cho: 8g, Fat: 0g, Na: 4mg, Pro: 1g

Watermelon and Basil Smoothie

Servings: 2
Prep Time: 5 minutes
Cook Time: 0 minutes

Ingredients:

1. 2 cups watermelon, cubed (300g)
2. 1/4 cup fresh basil leaves (6g)
3. 1/2 cup ice cubes

Instructions:

4. Place watermelon, basil leaves, and ice cubes in a blender.
5. Blend until smooth and frothy.
6. Pour into glasses and serve immediately for a cool and aromatic summer treat.

Nutritional Information: Kcal: 45, Cho: 11g, Fat: 0.5g, Na: 3mg, Pro: 1g

Kiwi and Spinach Juice

Servings: 2
Prep Time: 5 minutes
Cook Time: 0 minutes

Ingredients:

1. 3 kiwis, peeled and sliced (270g)
2. 1 cup spinach leaves (30g)
3. 1 cup water (240ml)

Instructions:

4. Combine kiwi slices, spinach leaves, and water in a blender.
5. Blend on high until the juice is smooth.
6. Strain through a fine mesh sieve to remove any fibers, if preferred.
7. Serve immediately, enjoying the vibrant green color and the rich nutrients.

Nutritional Information: Kcal: 90, Cho: 21g, Fat: 1g, Na: 20mg, Pro: 2g

CHAPTER 9:
Dinner Recipes

MAIN DISHES: FULL EVENING FARE

Grilled Turkey Breast with Cauliflower Mash

Servings: 2
Prep Time: 10 minutes
Cook Time: 20 minutes

Ingredients:
1. 1 turkey breast, boneless and skinless (400g)
2. 1 head cauliflower, cut into florets (600g)
3. 2 tablespoons olive oil (30ml)
4. Salt and pepper to taste

Instructions:
5. Preheat grill to medium-high heat (375°F or 190°C).
6. Brush turkey breast with 1 tablespoon olive oil and season with salt and pepper.
7. Grill turkey breast for 10 minutes on each side or until fully cooked.
8. Meanwhile, steam cauliflower florets until tender, about 15 minutes.
9. Mash the steamed cauliflower with remaining olive oil and season with salt and pepper.
10. Serve grilled turkey over the cauliflower mash.

Nutritional Information: Kcal: 310, Cho: 12g, Fat: 10g, Na: 200mg, Pro: 46g

Seared Cod with Broccoli and Almonds

Servings: 2
Prep Time: 5 minutes
Cook Time: 15 minutes

Ingredients:
1. 2 cod fillets (300g)

2. 2 cups broccoli florets (200g)
3. 2 tablespoons slivered almonds (15g)
4. 1 tablespoon olive oil (15ml)
5. Salt and pepper to taste

Instructions:

6. Heat olive oil in a skillet over medium heat (350°F or 177°C).
7. Season cod fillets with salt and pepper, then sear for about 4 minutes on each side or until cooked through.
8. In another pan, sauté broccoli florets until tender and stir in almonds.
9. Serve the seared cod with broccoli and almonds.

Nutritional Information: Kcal: 255, Cho: 8g, Fat: 11g, Na: 190mg, Pro: 34g

Lemon Garlic Shrimp over Zucchini Noodles

Servings: 2
Prep Time: 10 minutes
Cook Time: 10 minutes

Ingredients:

1. 12 large shrimp, peeled and deveined (200g)
2. 2 zucchinis, spiralized (400g)
3. 2 cloves garlic, minced (6g)
4. Juice of 1 lemon (30ml)
5. 1 tablespoon olive oil (15ml)
6. Salt and pepper to taste

Instructions:

7. Heat olive oil in a pan over medium heat (350°F or 177°C).
8. Add garlic and shrimp, season with salt and pepper, and sauté until shrimp are pink and cooked through, about 5 minutes.
9. Remove from heat and stir in lemon juice.
10. Toss shrimp with spiralized zucchini noodles and serve immediately.

Nutritional Information: Kcal: 200, Cho: 8g, Fat: 8g, Na: 220mg, Pro: 24g

Lamb Chops with Mint Pesto

Servings: 2
Prep Time: 10 minutes
Cook Time: 10 minutes

Ingredients:

1. 4 lamb chops (400g)
2. 1/2 cup fresh mint leaves (12g)
3. 1/4 cup almonds, toasted (30g)
4. 2 tablespoons olive oil (30ml)
5. 1 garlic clove (3g)
6. Salt and pepper to taste

Instructions:

7. Season lamb chops with salt and pepper.
8. Grill over medium-high heat (375°F or 190°C) for about 5 minutes on each side.
9. For the pesto, blend mint leaves, almonds, olive oil, and garlic until smooth.
10. Serve grilled lamb chops drizzled with mint pesto.

Nutritional Information: Kcal: 375, Cho: 3g, Fat: 25g, Na: 220mg, Pro: 32g

Baked Chicken with Brussels Sprouts

Servings: 2
Prep Time: 5 minutes
Cook Time: 25 minutes

Ingredients:

1. 2 chicken breasts, boneless and skinless (400g)
2. 2 cups Brussels sprouts, halved (200g)
3. 1 tablespoon olive oil (15ml)
4. Salt and pepper to taste

Instructions:

5. Preheat oven to 400°F (204°C).
6. Toss Brussels sprouts with olive oil, salt, and pepper, and spread on a baking sheet.
7. Season chicken breasts and place them on the same baking sheet.
8. Bake for 25 minutes or until chicken is cooked through and Brussels sprouts are caramelized.
9. Serve hot, with extra seasoning if desired.

Nutritional Information: Kcal: 290, Cho: 10g, Fat: 10g, Na: 220mg, Pro: 39g

Herb-Roasted Pork Tenderloin

Servings: 2
Prep Time: 10 minutes
Cook Time: 25 minutes

Ingredients:

1. 1 pork tenderloin (500g)
2. 2 tablespoons fresh rosemary, chopped (6g)
3. 2 tablespoons fresh thyme, chopped (6g)
4. 2 cloves garlic, minced (6g)
5. 1 tablespoon olive oil (15ml)
6. Salt and pepper to taste

Instructions:

7. Preheat oven to 400°F (204°C).
8. Rub the pork tenderloin with olive oil, then coat evenly with garlic, rosemary, thyme, salt, and pepper.
9. Place the tenderloin in a roasting pan.
10. Roast in the preheated oven for 25 minutes or until a thermometer inserted into the thickest part reads 145°F (63°C).
11. Let rest for 5 minutes before slicing and serving.

Nutritional Information: Kcal: 310, Cho: 1g, Fat: 14g, Na: 75mg, Pro: 42g

Beef and Broccoli Stir Fry

Servings: 2
Prep Time: 10 minutes
Cook Time: 10 minutes

Ingredients:

1. 1/2 pound beef sirloin, thinly sliced (225g)
2. 2 cups broccoli florets (200g)
3. 1 onion, sliced (110g)
4. 2 tablespoons soy sauce (30ml)
5. 1 tablespoon sesame oil (15ml)
6. 1 garlic clove, minced (3g)
7. Salt and pepper to taste

Instructions:

8. Heat sesame oil in a large skillet over medium-high heat (350°F or 177°C).
9. Add garlic and onion, sauté until onion is translucent.
10. Add beef slices, stir-fry until browned and nearly cooked through.
11. Add broccoli and soy sauce, continue to stir-fry until broccoli is tender and beef is fully cooked.
12. Season with salt and pepper, serve immediately.

Nutritional Information: Kcal: 275, Cho: 11g, Fat: 16g, Na: 630mg, Pro: 26g

Spicy Grilled Tuna Steaks

Servings: 2
Prep Time: 5 minutes
Cook Time: 8 minutes

Ingredients:

1. 2 tuna steaks (400g)
2. 1 tablespoon olive oil (15ml)
3. 1 teaspoon chili flakes (2g)
4. Juice of 1 lemon (30ml)
5. Salt and pepper to taste

Instructions:

6. Preheat grill to high heat (450°F or 232°C).
7. Brush tuna steaks with olive oil and sprinkle with chili flakes, salt, and pepper.
8. Grill for about 4 minutes on each side for medium-rare or until desired doneness.
9. Squeeze fresh lemon juice over the cooked tuna before serving.
10. Serve hot, garnished with additional lemon slices if desired.

Nutritional Information: Kcal: 290, Cho: 0g, Fat: 13g, Na: 125mg, Pro: 39g

Stuffed Bell Peppers with Quinoa and Vegetables

Servings: 2
Prep Time: 15 minutes
Cook Time: 30 minutes

Ingredients:

1. 2 bell peppers, halved and seeded (300g)
2. 1/2 cup cooked quinoa (85g)
3. 1/2 cup diced zucchini (60g)
4. 1/2 cup diced mushrooms (75g)
5. 1/4 cup diced red onion (40g)
6. 1 clove garlic, minced (3g)
7. 1 tablespoon olive oil (15ml)
8. Salt and pepper to taste

Instructions:

9. Preheat oven to 375°F (190°C).
10. Heat olive oil in a skillet over medium heat. Add garlic, onion, zucchini, and mushrooms. Sauté until vegetables are tender.
11. Stir in cooked quinoa and season with salt and pepper.
12. Stuff the bell pepper halves with the quinoa mixture.
13. Place stuffed peppers in a baking dish and cover with foil.
14. Bake for 30 minutes or until peppers are tender.

Nutritional Information: Kcal: 220, Cho: 27g, Fat: 10g, Na: 75mg, Pro: 6g

Eggplant and Tomato Stew

Servings: 2
Prep Time: 10 minutes
Cook Time: 25 minutes

Ingredients:

1. 1 large eggplant, cubed (300g)
2. 2 tomatoes, chopped (200g)
3. 1 onion, chopped (110g)
4. 2 cloves garlic, minced (6g)
5. 1 tablespoon olive oil (15ml)
6. 1 teaspoon dried basil (1g)
7. Salt and pepper to taste

Instructions:

8. Heat olive oil in a large pot over medium heat. Add onion and garlic, sauté until soft.
9. Add eggplant and cook until it begins to soften.
10. Stir in tomatoes and basil, season with salt and pepper.
11. Cover and simmer for 20 minutes or until all vegetables are tender.
12. Serve hot.

Nutritional Information: Kcal: 180, Cho: 24g, Fat: 9g, Na: 75mg, Pro: 4g

Baked Sole with Lemon and Dill

Servings: 2
Prep Time: 5 minutes
Cook Time: 15 minutes

Ingredients:

1. 2 sole fillets (350g)
2. Juice of 1 lemon (30ml)
3. 1 tablespoon chopped fresh dill (3g)
4. 1 tablespoon olive oil (15ml)
5. Salt and pepper to taste

Instructions:

6. Preheat oven to 375°F (190°C).
7. Place sole fillets on a baking sheet lined with parchment paper.
8. Drizzle with olive oil and lemon juice. Sprinkle with dill, salt, and pepper.
9. Bake for 15 minutes or until fish flakes easily with a fork.
10. Serve immediately.

Nutritional Information: Kcal: 210, Cho: 0g, Fat: 9g, Na: 125mg, Pro: 30g

Turkey Lettuce Wraps

Servings: 2
Prep Time: 10 minutes
Cook Time: 10 minutes

Ingredients:

1. 1/2 pound ground turkey (225g)
2. 1 tablespoon soy sauce (15ml)
3. 1 teaspoon sesame oil (5ml)
4. 1 clove garlic, minced (3g)
5. 1/2 cup chopped water chestnuts (75g)
6. 6 leaves of romaine or butter lettuce (90g)
7. Salt and pepper to taste

Instructions:

8. Heat sesame oil in a skillet over medium heat. Add garlic and ground turkey. Cook until turkey is browned.
9. Stir in soy sauce and water chestnuts. Cook for another 5 minutes.
10. Spoon the turkey mixture into lettuce leaves.
11. Serve immediately.

Nutritional Information: Kcal: 190, Cho: 8g, Fat: 10g, Na: 530mg, Pro: 20g

Tuna Salad with Avocado

Servings: 2
Prep Time: 10 minutes
Cook Time: 0 minutes

Ingredients:

1. 1 can tuna, drained (120g)
2. 1 ripe avocado, diced (200g)
3. 1/4 cup diced celery (30g)
4. 1 tablespoon lemon juice (15ml)
5. 1 tablespoon olive oil (15ml)
6. Salt and pepper to taste

Instructions:

7. In a bowl, mix together the tuna, avocado, celery, lemon juice, and olive oil.
8. Season with salt and pepper to taste.
9. Chill in the refrigerator for 10 minutes before serving.

Nutritional Information: Kcal: 280, Cho: 8g, Fat: 20g, Na: 300mg, Pro: 20g

Chickpea and Spinach Curry

Servings: 2
Prep Time: 10 minutes
Cook Time: 20 minutes

Ingredients:

1. 1 can chickpeas, drained and rinsed (240g)
2. 2 cups spinach leaves (60g)
3. 1 onion, diced (110g)
4. 2 cloves garlic, minced (6g)
5. 1 tablespoon curry powder (6g)
6. 1 teaspoon ground cumin (2g)
7. 1 cup canned diced tomatoes (240ml)
8. 1/2 cup coconut milk (120ml)
9. 1 tablespoon olive oil (15ml)
10. Salt to taste

Instructions:

11. Heat olive oil in a skillet over medium heat. Sauté onion and garlic until soft.
12. Stir in curry powder and cumin, cooking for 1 minute.
13. Add chickpeas and tomatoes, bring to a simmer.
14. Stir in spinach and coconut milk, continue to cook until spinach is wilted and curry is heated through.
15. Season with salt, serve warm.

Nutritional Information: Kcal: 295, Cho: 33g, Fat: 14g, Na: 480mg, Pro: 10g

Grilled Asparagus and Poached Egg

Servings: 2
Prep Time: 5 minutes
Cook Time: 10 minutes

Ingredients:

1. 1 bunch asparagus, trimmed (200g)
2. 2 eggs
3. 1 tablespoon olive oil (15ml)
4. Salt and pepper to taste
5. 1 teaspoon vinegar (5ml)

Instructions:

6. Preheat grill to medium-high heat. Brush asparagus with olive oil and season with salt and pepper.
7. Grill asparagus until tender and charred, about 5 minutes.
8. Meanwhile, bring water to a gentle simmer in a saucepan, add vinegar. Carefully crack eggs into the water and poach for about 3 minutes.
9. Remove eggs with a slotted spoon and drain.
10. Serve poached eggs over grilled asparagus.

Nutritional Information: Kcal: 180, Cho: 4g, Fat: 14g, Na: 190mg, Pro: 12g

Caprese Salad with Balsamic Reduction

Servings: 2
Prep Time: 5 minutes
Cook Time: 10 minutes

Ingredients:

1. 2 large tomatoes, sliced (400g)
2. 8 ounces fresh mozzarella cheese, sliced (225g)
3. 1/4 cup fresh basil leaves (6g)
4. 2 tablespoons balsamic vinegar (30ml)
5. 1 tablespoon olive oil (15ml)
6. Salt and pepper to taste

Instructions:

7. Arrange tomato and mozzarella slices on a platter, alternating and overlapping them.
8. Scatter basil leaves over the top.
9. In a small saucepan, simmer balsamic vinegar over low heat until reduced by half.
10. Drizzle olive oil and the reduced balsamic over the salad.
11. Season with salt and pepper to taste.

Nutritional Information: Kcal: 340, Cho: 12g, Fat: 25g, Na: 420mg, Pro: 22g

Thai Beef Salad

Servings: 2
Prep Time: 15 minutes
Cook Time: 10 minutes

Ingredients:

1. 8 oz beef sirloin, thinly sliced (225g)
2. 2 cups mixed salad greens (60g)
3. 1/2 cup cherry tomatoes, halved (75g)
4. 1/4 cup red onion, thinly sliced (40g)
5. 1/4 cup fresh cilantro, chopped (15g)
6. 1/4 cup fresh mint leaves (15g)
7. 1 tablespoon fish sauce (15ml)
8. 1 tablespoon lime juice (15ml)
9. 1 tablespoon soy sauce (15ml)
10. 1 teaspoon honey (5ml)
11. 1 red chili, sliced (optional) (5g)
12. 1 tablespoon olive oil (15ml)

Instructions:

13. Heat olive oil in a skillet over medium-high heat. Add sliced beef and cook until browned, about 3-4 minutes per side.
14. In a small bowl, whisk together fish sauce, lime juice, soy sauce, and honey.
15. In a large bowl, combine salad greens, cherry tomatoes, red onion, cilantro, and mint.
16. Add cooked beef to the salad. Drizzle with the dressing and toss to combine.
17. Garnish with sliced red chili, if desired. Serve immediately.

Nutritional Information: Kcal: 320, Cho: 15g, Fat: 20g, Na: 900mg, Pro: 25g

Indian Chicken Curry with Cauliflower Rice

Servings: 2
Prep Time: 15 minutes
Cook Time: 25 minutes

Ingredients:

1. 1 chicken breast, diced (200g)
2. 1 cup cauliflower, grated into rice (150g)
3. 1/2 cup diced tomatoes (120g)
4. 1/2 cup coconut milk (120ml)
5. 1 small onion, diced (70g)
6. 2 cloves garlic, minced (6g)
7. 1 tablespoon curry powder (6g)
8. 1 teaspoon ground cumin (2g)
9. 1 teaspoon ground turmeric (2g)
10. 1 tablespoon olive oil (15ml)
11. Salt to taste

Instructions:

12. Heat olive oil in a skillet over medium heat. Sauté onion and garlic until soft.
13. Add curry powder, cumin, and turmeric, and cook for 1 minute.
14. Add diced chicken and cook until no longer pink, about 5-7 minutes.
15. Stir in diced tomatoes and coconut milk. Simmer for 10 minutes.
16. Meanwhile, steam the grated cauliflower until tender, about 5 minutes.
17. Serve the curry over the cauliflower rice.

Nutritional Information: Kcal: 350, Cho: 18g, Fat: 18g, Na: 250mg, Pro: 28g

Moroccan Lentil Soup

Servings: 2
Prep Time: 10 minutes
Cook Time: 30 minutes

Ingredients:

1. 1/2 cup dried lentils, rinsed (100g)
2. 1 small carrot, diced (60g)
3. 1 small onion, diced (70g)
4. 1 celery stalk, diced (50g)
5. 2 cloves garlic, minced (6g)
6. 1 can diced tomatoes (14.5 oz) (411g)
7. 2 cups vegetable broth (480ml)
8. 1 teaspoon ground cumin (2g)
9. 1 teaspoon ground coriander (2g)

10. 1/2 teaspoon ground cinnamon (1g)
11. 1 tablespoon olive oil (15ml)
12. Salt and pepper to taste

Instructions:

13. Heat olive oil in a large pot over medium heat. Sauté onion, garlic, carrot, and celery until softened.
14. Stir in cumin, coriander, and cinnamon, and cook for 1 minute.
15. Add lentils, diced tomatoes, and vegetable broth. Bring to a boil.
16. Reduce heat and simmer for 25-30 minutes, until lentils are tender.
17. Season with salt and pepper. Serve hot.

Nutritional Information: Kcal: 250, Cho: 40g, Fat: 6g, Na: 600mg, Pro: 12g

Japanese Miso Soup with Tofu

Servings: 2
Prep Time: 5 minutes
Cook Time: 10 minutes

Ingredients:

1. 4 cups water (960ml)
2. 2 tablespoons miso paste (30g)
3. 1/2 cup tofu, cubed (100g)
4. 1/4 cup green onions, sliced (25g)
5. 1/4 cup seaweed, rehydrated (10g)

Instructions:

6. Bring water to a boil in a pot. Reduce heat to low and whisk in miso paste until dissolved.
7. Add tofu cubes and simmer for 5 minutes.
8. Stir in green onions and rehydrated seaweed. Cook for an additional 2 minutes.
9. Serve hot.

Nutritional Information: Kcal: 80, Cho: 8g, Fat: 3g, Na: 700mg, Pro: 6g

Italian Zucchini Pasta

Servings: 2
Prep Time: 10 minutes
Cook Time: 5 minutes

Ingredients:

1. 2 medium zucchinis, spiralized (300g)
2. 1 cup cherry tomatoes, halved (150g)

3. 2 cloves garlic, minced (6g)
4. 1/4 cup fresh basil leaves, chopped (10g)
5. 2 tablespoons olive oil (30ml)
6. 1/4 teaspoon red pepper flakes (optional) (1g)
7. Salt and pepper to taste

Instructions:

8. Heat olive oil in a large skillet over medium heat.
9. Add minced garlic and red pepper flakes, sauté for 1 minute until fragrant.
10. Add spiralized zucchini and cherry tomatoes to the skillet. Cook for 2-3 minutes until zucchini is tender but not mushy.
11. Stir in chopped basil and season with salt and pepper.
12. Serve immediately, garnished with extra basil if desired.

Nutritional Information: Kcal: 180, Cho: 14g, Fat: 14g, Na: 10mg, Pro: 3g

Greek Stuffed Tomatoes

Servings: 2
Prep Time: 15 minutes
Cook Time: 25 minutes

Ingredients:

1. 4 medium tomatoes, tops cut off and insides scooped out (500g)
2. 1/2 cup cooked quinoa (90g)
3. 1/4 cup crumbled feta cheese (40g)
4. 1/4 cup chopped cucumber (40g)
5. 1/4 cup chopped red onion (30g)
6. 1/4 cup chopped kalamata olives (30g)
7. 1 tablespoon olive oil (15ml)
8. 1 tablespoon lemon juice (15ml)
9. 1 teaspoon dried oregano (1g)
10. Salt and pepper to taste

Instructions:

11. Preheat oven to 375°F (190°C).
12. In a bowl, mix cooked quinoa, feta cheese, cucumber, red onion, olives, olive oil, lemon juice, and oregano. Season with salt and pepper.
13. Stuff the hollowed tomatoes with the quinoa mixture.
14. Place the stuffed tomatoes in a baking dish and bake for 20-25 minutes until tomatoes are tender.
15. Serve warm.

Nutritional Information: Kcal: 250, Cho: 30g, Fat: 12g, Na: 480mg, Pro: 7g

Spanish Gazpacho

Servings: 2
Prep Time: 15 minutes
Cook Time: 0 minutes

Ingredients:

1. 4 ripe tomatoes, chopped (500g)
2. 1 cucumber, peeled and chopped (200g)
3. 1 red bell pepper, chopped (150g)
4. 1 small red onion, chopped (70g)
5. 2 cloves garlic, minced (6g)
6. 2 tablespoons olive oil (30ml)
7. 2 tablespoons red wine vinegar (30ml)
8. 1 cup cold water (240ml)
9. Salt and pepper to taste

Instructions:

10. Combine tomatoes, cucumber, bell pepper, red onion, and garlic in a blender.
11. Add olive oil, red wine vinegar, and cold water. Blend until smooth.
12. Season with salt and pepper to taste.
13. Chill in the refrigerator for at least 2 hours before serving.
14. Serve cold, garnished with extra chopped vegetables if desired.

Nutritional Information: Kcal: 180, Cho: 22g, Fat: 10g, Na: 20mg, Pro: 3g

Vietnamese Spring Rolls

Servings: 2
Prep Time: 20 minutes
Cook Time: 0 minutes

Ingredients:

1. 4 rice paper wrappers (40g)
2. 1 cup cooked shrimp, sliced in half lengthwise (100g)
3. 1/2 cup shredded lettuce (30g)
4. 1/2 cup julienned carrots (60g)
5. 1/2 cup bean sprouts (50g)
6. 1/4 cup fresh cilantro leaves (10g)
7. 1/4 cup fresh mint leaves (10g)
8. 1/4 cup fresh basil leaves (10g)
9. 1/4 cup rice vermicelli, cooked (30g)

Instructions:

10. Fill a large bowl with warm water. Dip one rice paper wrapper into the water for about 5 seconds to soften.

11. Lay the softened wrapper flat on a clean surface. In a row across the center, place 2 shrimp halves, a handful of lettuce, carrots, bean sprouts, cilantro, mint, basil, and a small amount of rice vermicelli.

12. Fold the sides inward over the filling, then roll tightly from the bottom to the top.

13. Repeat with the remaining wrappers and fillings.

14. Serve with your favorite dipping sauce.

Nutritional Information: Kcal: 200, Cho: 30g, Fat: 2g, Na: 250mg, Pro: 15g

CHAPTER 10:
Dessert Recipes

FRUIT-BASED: NATURAL SWEETNESS

Baked Apples with Cinnamon

Servings: 2
Prep Time: 10 minutes
Cook Time: 30 minutes

Ingredients:
1. 2 large apples, cored (360g)
2. 2 teaspoons cinnamon (4g)
3. 1 tablespoon honey (15ml)
4. 1/4 cup walnuts, chopped (30g)

Instructions:
5. Preheat oven to 350°F (177°C).
6. Place apples in a baking dish.
7. Mix honey and cinnamon together in a small bowl.
8. Spoon the cinnamon-honey mixture into the center of each apple and top with chopped walnuts.
9. Bake in the preheated oven for 30 minutes or until apples are tender.
10. Serve warm.

Nutritional Information: Kcal: 195, Cho: 31g, Fat: 8g, Na: 2mg, Pro: 2g

Mango and Coconut Rice

Servings: 2
Prep Time: 5 minutes
Cook Time: 20 minutes

Ingredients:

1. 1 cup jasmine rice (185g)
2. 1 cup coconut milk (240ml)
3. 1/2 cup water (120ml)
4. 1 ripe mango, diced (200g)
5. 1 tablespoon shredded coconut (6g)

Instructions:

6. Rinse jasmine rice under cold water until the water runs clear.
7. In a saucepan, combine rice, coconut milk, and water. Bring to a boil.
8. Reduce heat to low, cover, and simmer for 18 minutes or until rice is tender.
9. Fluff rice with a fork and gently stir in diced mango.
10. Sprinkle with shredded coconut before serving.

Nutritional Information: Kcal: 330, Cho: 53g, Fat: 11g, Na: 15mg, Pro: 5g

Fruit Salad with Citrus Mint Dressing

Servings: 2
Prep Time: 10 minutes
Cook Time: 0 minutes

Ingredients:

1. 1 cup strawberries, halved (152g)
2. 1 cup blueberries (148g)
3. 1 kiwi, peeled and sliced (90g)
4. Juice of 1 orange (60ml)
5. 1 tablespoon chopped mint (1g)

Instructions:

6. In a large bowl, combine strawberries, blueberries, and kiwi.
7. In a small bowl, whisk together orange juice and chopped mint.
8. Pour the dressing over the fruit and toss gently to coat.
9. Chill in the refrigerator for 10 minutes before serving to allow flavors to meld.

Nutritional Information: Kcal: 120, Cho: 29g, Fat: 1g, Na: 3mg, Pro: 2g

Grilled Pineapple with Honey and Lime

Servings: 2
Prep Time: 5 minutes
Cook Time: 10 minutes

Ingredients:
1. 4 pineapple rings (200g)
2. 1 tablespoon honey (15ml)
3. Juice of 1 lime (15ml)

Instructions:
4. Preheat grill to medium heat.
5. Brush pineapple rings with honey and drizzle with lime juice.
6. Grill pineapple for about 5 minutes on each side or until grill marks appear and the pineapple is heated through.
7. Serve warm.

Nutritional Information: Kcal: 110, Cho: 27g, Fat: 0g, Na: 1mg, Pro: 1g

Berries with Whipped Coconut Cream

Servings: 2
Prep Time: 10 minutes
Cook Time: 0 minutes

Ingredients:
1. 1 cup mixed berries (strawberries, blueberries, raspberries) (150g)
2. 1/2 cup coconut cream, chilled (120ml)
3. 1 tablespoon powdered sugar (8g)

Instructions:
4. In a bowl, whip chilled coconut cream with powdered sugar until soft peaks form.
5. Serve mixed berries topped with a dollop of whipped coconut cream.

Nutritional Information: Kcal: 180, Cho: 18g, Fat: 12g, Na: 4mg, Pro: 2g

Pear and Vanilla Compote

Servings: 2
Prep Time: 5 minutes
Cook Time: 15 minutes

Ingredients:

1. 2 pears, peeled, cored, and diced (360g)
2. 1 vanilla bean, split and seeds scraped (or 1 teaspoon vanilla extract) (5ml)
3. 1 tablespoon honey (15ml)
4. 1/2 cup water (120ml)

Instructions:

5. Combine pears, vanilla bean seeds (and pod if using), honey, and water in a small saucepan.
6. Bring to a simmer over medium heat, then reduce heat to low.
7. Cook gently, stirring occasionally, until pears are soft and the liquid has thickened, about 15 minutes.
8. Remove from heat and let cool slightly. Remove vanilla pod if used.
9. Serve warm or chilled.

Nutritional Information: Kcal: 120, Cho: 31g, Fat: 0g, Na: 2mg, Pro: 0g

Roasted Peaches with Nutmeg

Servings: 2
Prep Time: 5 minutes
Cook Time: 25 minutes

Ingredients:

1. 2 peaches, halved and pitted (300g)
2. 1/4 teaspoon ground nutmeg (0.5g)
3. 1 tablespoon honey (15ml)

Instructions:

4. Preheat oven to 375°F (190°C).
5. Place peach halves cut-side up on a baking sheet.
6. Drizzle with honey and sprinkle with nutmeg.
7. Roast in the oven until peaches are tender and juicy, about 25 minutes.
8. Serve warm, perhaps with a dollop of yogurt if desired.

Nutritional Information: Kcal: 85, Cho: 21g, Fat: 0.5g, Na: 0mg, Pro: 1g

Strawberry and Basil Sorbet

Servings: 2
Prep Time: 10 minutes (plus freezing time)
Cook Time: 5 minutes

Ingredients:

1. 2 cups strawberries, hulled (300g)
2. 1/4 cup fresh basil leaves (6g)
3. 1/4 cup sugar (50g)
4. 1/2 cup water (120ml)

Instructions:

5. In a small saucepan, combine sugar and water. Bring to a boil, stirring until sugar dissolves. Allow to cool.
6. In a blender, puree strawberries, basil, and the cooled sugar syrup until smooth.
7. Pour the mixture into an ice cream maker and churn according to manufacturer's instructions, or freeze in a shallow dish, stirring every half hour until frozen.
8. Serve immediately for a soft texture or freeze until firm.

Nutritional Information: Kcal: 160, Cho: 40g, Fat: 0.5g, Na: 3mg, Pro: 1g

Dark Chocolate Avocado Mousse

Servings: 2
Prep Time: 10 minutes
Cook Time: 0 minutes

Ingredients:

1. 1 ripe avocado, peeled and pitted (200g)
2. 2 tablespoons unsweetened cocoa powder (10g)
3. 2 tablespoons honey (30ml)
4. 1/2 teaspoon vanilla extract (2ml)

Instructions:

5. In a blender, combine the avocado, cocoa powder, honey, and vanilla extract.
6. Blend until smooth and creamy.
7. Divide the mousse into two serving dishes.
8. Chill in the refrigerator for at least 30 minutes before serving.

Nutritional Information: Kcal: 240, Cho: 30g, Fat: 15g, Na: 10mg, Pro: 3g

Almond Flour Lemon Cake

Servings: 2
Prep Time: 15 minutes
Cook Time: 30 minutes

Ingredients:

1. 1 cup almond flour (96g)
2. 2 tablespoons honey (30ml)
3. 2 eggs
4. 1 lemon, zested and juiced (45ml)
5. 1/2 teaspoon baking powder (2g)

Instructions:

6. Preheat oven to 350°F (177°C).
7. In a bowl, mix together almond flour, baking powder, lemon zest, and lemon juice.
8. Stir in eggs and honey until well combined.

9. Pour the batter into a greased loaf pan or round cake pan.
10. Bake for 30 minutes or until a toothpick inserted into the center comes out clean.
11. Let cool before slicing.

Nutritional Information: Kcal: 280, Cho: 20g, Fat: 20g, Na: 120mg, Pro: 10g

Baked Peaches with Vanilla

Servings: 2
Prep Time: 5 minutes
Cook Time: 15 minutes

Ingredients:
1. 2 peaches, halved and pitted (300g)
2. 1/2 teaspoon vanilla extract (2ml)
3. 1 tablespoon honey (15ml)

Instructions:
4. Preheat oven to 375°F (190°C).
5. Place peach halves cut-side up on a baking sheet.
6. Drizzle with honey and vanilla extract.
7. Bake for 15 minutes or until peaches are tender and juicy.
8. Serve warm, optionally with a dollop of Greek yogurt.

Nutritional Information: Kcal: 90, Cho: 21g, Fat: 0.5g, Na: 0mg, Pro: 1g

Coconut Flour Brownies

Servings: 2
Prep Time: 10 minutes
Cook Time: 20 minutes

Ingredients:
1. 1/4 cup coconut flour (30g)
2. 2 tablespoons unsweetened cocoa powder (10g)
3. 2 tablespoons coconut oil, melted (30ml)
4. 3 tablespoons honey (45ml)
5. 2 eggs
6. 1/2 teaspoon vanilla extract (2ml)

Instructions:
7. Preheat oven to 350°F (177°C).
8. In a bowl, combine coconut flour and cocoa powder.
9. Mix in coconut oil, honey, eggs, and vanilla until well combined.
10. Pour the batter into a greased square baking dish.
11. Bake for 20 minutes or until a toothpick inserted into the center comes out clean.
12. Let cool before cutting into squares.

Nutritional Information: Kcal: 280, Cho: 34g, Fat: 14g, Na: 65mg, Pro: 6g

Peanut Butter Protein Balls

Servings: 2
Prep Time: 10 minutes
Cook Time: 0 minutes

Ingredients:

1. 1/2 cup rolled oats (40g)
2. 1/4 cup natural peanut butter (60g)
3. 2 tablespoons honey (30ml)
4. 1 tablespoon chia seeds (10g)
5. 1/4 cup protein powder, vanilla flavor (30g)

Instructions:

6. In a mixing bowl, combine rolled oats, peanut butter, honey, chia seeds, and protein powder.
7. Stir until all ingredients are well mixed and the mixture begins to stick together.
8. Roll the mixture into small balls, about the size of a walnut.
9. Place the protein balls on a plate and refrigerate for at least 30 minutes to set.
10. Serve chilled as a nutritious snack.

Nutritional Information: Kcal: 280, Cho: 30g, Fat: 14g, Na: 70mg, Pro: 10g

Lemon and Blueberry Bars

Servings: 2
Prep Time: 15 minutes
Cook Time: 20 minutes

Ingredients:

1. 1 cup fresh blueberries (148g)
2. 1/2 cup almond flour (48g)
3. 2 eggs
4. 1/4 cup honey (60ml)
5. 1 lemon, zest and juice (45ml)

Instructions:

6. Preheat oven to 350°F (177°C).
7. In a bowl, mix almond flour, eggs, honey, and lemon zest and juice until smooth.
8. Fold in blueberries gently.
9. Pour the mixture into a greased 8x8 inch baking dish.
10. Bake for 20 minutes or until the edges are golden and a toothpick inserted in the center comes out clean.
11. Cool before cutting into bars and serve.

Nutritional Information: Kcal: 295, Cho: 35g, Fat: 14g, Na: 70mg, Pro: 8g

Flourless Chocolate Chip Cookies

Servings: 2
Prep Time: 10 minutes
Cook Time: 12 minutes

Ingredients:

1. 1 cup almond butter (240g)
2. 1/3 cup sugar substitute, such as erythritol (70g)
3. 1 egg
4. 1/2 cup dark chocolate chips, sugar-free (90g)
5. 1 teaspoon vanilla extract (5ml)

Instructions:

6. Preheat oven to 350°F (177°C).
7. In a bowl, combine almond butter, sugar substitute, egg, and vanilla extract. Mix until smooth.
8. Stir in chocolate chips.
9. Drop spoonfuls of the cookie dough onto a parchment-lined baking sheet.
10. Bake for 12 minutes or until the edges start to turn golden.
11. Remove from oven and let cool on the baking sheet for a few minutes before transferring to a cooling rack.

Nutritional Information: Kcal: 280, Cho: 20g, Fat: 21g, Na: 55mg, Pro: 9g

NON-DAIRY DELIGHTS: INCLUSIVE AND HORMONE-FRIENDLY

Vegan Chocolate Gelato

Servings: 2
Prep Time: 10 minutes
Cook Time: 0 minutes (plus several hours freezing)

Ingredients:

1. 2 bananas, sliced and frozen (240g)
2. 1/4 cup unsweetened cocoa powder (20g)
3. 1/2 cup coconut milk (120ml)
4. 1 tablespoon maple syrup (15ml)

Instructions:

5. Place the frozen banana slices, cocoa powder, coconut milk, and maple syrup in a blender.
6. Blend on high until smooth and creamy, scraping down the sides as needed.
7. Pour the mixture into a shallow container.
8. Freeze until solid, about 4-6 hours.
9. Before serving, let sit at room temperature for 5-10 minutes to soften slightly for scooping.

Nutritional Information: Kcal: 245, Cho: 52g, Fat: 7g, Na: 5mg, Pro: 3g

Cashew Cheese with Figs

Servings: 2
Prep Time: 15 minutes (plus soaking time)
Cook Time: 0 minutes

Ingredients:

1. 1 cup raw cashews, soaked for 4 hours then drained (150g)
2. 4 dried figs, chopped (60g)
3. 2 tablespoons nutritional yeast (10g)
4. 1 garlic clove, minced (3g)
5. Juice of 1 lemon (30ml)
6. Salt to taste

Instructions:

7. In a food processor, combine soaked cashews, nutritional yeast, minced garlic, lemon juice, and salt.
8. Process until smooth and creamy.
9. Stir in chopped figs by hand.

 GALVESTON DIET COOKBOOK FOR BEGINNERS

10. Refrigerate for at least 1 hour to allow flavors to meld and the mixture to firm up.
11. Serve with crackers or sliced vegetables.

Nutritional Information: Kcal: 370, Cho: 38g, Fat: 22g, Na: 10mg, Pro: 12g

Banana Ice Cream

Servings: 2
Prep Time: 5 minutes
Cook Time: 0 minutes (plus freezing time)

Ingredients:
1. 3 bananas, peeled, sliced, and frozen (360g)

Instructions:
2. Place frozen banana slices into a food processor.
3. Pulse until the bananas break down into a smooth, creamy texture.
4. Continue processing until the mixture achieves the consistency of soft serve ice cream.
5. Serve immediately or freeze for a firmer texture.

Nutritional Information: Kcal: 105, Cho: 27g, Fat: 0g, Na: 1mg, Pro: 1g

Dairy-Free Raspberry Sorbet

Servings: 2
Prep Time: 10 minutes
Cook Time: 0 minutes (plus soaking time)

Ingredients:
1. 2 cups raspberries, frozen (250g)
2. 1/4 cup water (60ml)
3. 2 tablespoons honey (30ml)

Instructions:
4. Combine frozen raspberries, water, and honey in a blender.
5. Blend until smooth.
6. Pour the mixture into a shallow container.
7. Freeze until solid, about 3-4 hours, stirring every hour to break up ice crystals.
8. Before serving, process again briefly in the blender for a smoother texture.

Nutritional Information: Kcal: 140, Cho: 34g, Fat: 1g, Na: 2mg, Pro: 2g

Avocado Lime Cheesecake

Servings: 2
Prep Time: 15 minutes
Cook Time: 0 minutes (plus soaking time)

Ingredients:

1. 1 ripe avocado, peeled and pitted (200g)
2. 1/4 cup coconut cream (60ml)
3. 2 tablespoons lime juice (30ml)
4. 1/4 cup honey (60ml)
5. 1/2 cup crushed almonds for base (60g)
6. 1 tablespoon coconut oil, melted (15ml)

Instructions:

7. Mix crushed almonds and melted coconut oil in a small bowl. Press into the bottom of two serving dishes to form a base.
8. Blend avocado, coconut cream, lime juice, and honey in a blender until smooth.
9. Pour the avocado mixture over the almond base.
10. Refrigerate for at least 2 hours or until set.
11. Serve chilled, garnished with lime zest if desired.

Nutritional Information: Kcal: 480, Cho: 45g, Fat: 32g, Na: 10mg, Pro: 6g

Coconut Tapioca Pudding

Servings: 2
Prep Time: 5 minutes
Cook Time: 15 minutes

Ingredients:

1. 1/4 cup small pearl tapioca (50g)
2. 1 cup coconut milk (240ml)
3. 2 tablespoons honey (30ml)
4. 1/2 teaspoon vanilla extract (2ml)

Instructions:

5. Soak tapioca pearls in water for 30 minutes, then drain.
6. In a saucepan, combine soaked tapioca, coconut milk, and honey.
7. Cook over medium heat, stirring constantly, until the tapioca pearls become translucent and the pudding thickens, about 15 minutes.
8. Remove from heat, stir in vanilla extract.
9. Let cool slightly before serving warm, or chill in the refrigerator.

Nutritional Information: Kcal: 295, Cho: 42g, Fat: 12g, Na: 15mg, Pro: 2g

Almond Milk Rice Pudding

Servings: 2
Prep Time: 5 minutes
Cook Time: 25 minutes

Ingredients:

1. 1/2 cup cooked rice (90g)
2. 1 cup almond milk (240ml)
3. 1 tablespoon honey (15ml)
4. 1/2 teaspoon cinnamon (1g)
5. 1/4 teaspoon nutmeg (0.5g)

Instructions:

6. In a saucepan, combine cooked rice, almond milk, honey, cinnamon, and nutmeg.
7. Cook over medium-low heat, stirring frequently, until the mixture thickens and becomes creamy, about 25 minutes.
8. Remove from heat and let cool slightly.
9. Serve warm or chill in the refrigerator for a cold dessert.

Nutritional Information: Kcal: 180, Cho: 35g, Fat: 3g, Na: 50mg, Pro: 2g

Frozen Yogurt with Honey and Almonds

Servings: 2
Prep Time: 10 minutes
Cook Time: 0 minutes (plus freezing time)

Ingredients:

1. 1 cup Greek yogurt, non-fat (245g)
2. 2 tablespoons honey (30ml)
3. 1/4 cup sliced almonds, toasted (30g)

Instructions:

4. Mix Greek yogurt and honey in a bowl until well combined.
5. Pour the mixture into a shallow container and freeze until firm, about 2-3 hours.
6. Scoop the frozen yogurt into bowls.
7. Top with toasted almonds before serving.

Nutritional Information: Kcal: 230, Cho: 27g, Fat: 8g, Na: 55mg, Pro: 14g

PART III:

GALVESTON DIET LIFESTYLE

CHAPTER 11:
Adapting Recipes for Specific Health Needs

Cooking is more than just a daily chore; it's a powerful way to care for your health and well-being, especially when you're managing specific dietary needs. Whether you're contending with food allergies, dietary restrictions due to health conditions, or simply striving for a healthier lifestyle, the way you adapt your recipes can make a significant impact on your life. This chapter explores how to adjust recipes to meet various health needs without sacrificing flavor or enjoyment of food.

DIETARY ADJUSTMENTS FOR PERSONAL HEALTH CONCERNS

Understanding Nutritional Needs

The first step in adapting recipes for health is understanding the nutritional requirements of your specific condition. For instance, those with diabetes may need to focus on low-glycemic index foods that do not spike blood sugar levels, while individuals with heart conditions might prioritize low-sodium and low-fat ingredients to maintain cardiovascular health.

It's essential to research and sometimes consult with a nutritionist or healthcare provider to understand what adjustments will be most beneficial for you. This foundational knowledge not only helps in selecting the right ingredients but also in understanding the why behind these choices, empowering you to make informed decisions in the kitchen.

Substituting Ingredients

One of the simplest ways to adapt recipes is by substituting ingredients that better align with your health goals. Here are a few common substitutions:

- **Sugars:** Replace refined sugars with natural sweeteners like honey, maple syrup, or even pureed fruits such as bananas or apples to reduce refined sugar intake.
- **Fats:** Use healthier fats like avocado oil or coconut oil instead of butter or margarine. For baking, unsweetened applesauce or mashed bananas can often replace a significant portion of the fat without affecting the texture.
- **Dairy:** For those who are lactose intolerant or vegan, dairy can be replaced with almond milk, coconut milk, or other plant-based alternatives.
- **Flours:** Swap out white flour for whole grain, almond, or coconut flour to increase fiber content and reduce processed carbohydrate intake.

These substitutions not only make your meals healthier but can also introduce new flavors and textures, making your dining experience more enjoyable.

CREATIVE RECIPE MODIFICATIONS

Rethinking Cooking Methods

The method by which you prepare your food can significantly affect its healthiness. Grilling, baking, steaming, and sautéing are healthier cooking methods compared to frying. These techniques reduce the need for excess fat and preserve the nutrients in your food better than high-temperature methods like deep-frying.

Flavor Enhancement Without Excess Sodium

Many people need to reduce sodium intake for blood pressure management or other health reasons. Enhancing flavor without salt can be achieved through herbs, spices, citrus, vinegar, and other natural enhancers. Learning how to use these ingredients effectively can transform a bland dish into a culinary delight.

For example, a squeeze of fresh lemon juice can brighten up sautéed vegetables, while herbs like rosemary or thyme add a robust flavor to meats without the need for salt.

Portion Control

Adapting recipes isn't just about changing ingredients; it's also about adjusting portion sizes to meet dietary needs without feeling deprived. Using smaller plates, measuring serving sizes, and being mindful of the balance of macronutrients (proteins, fats, and carbohydrates) can help maintain a healthy diet and manage caloric intake.

IMPLEMENTING CHANGES GRADUALLY

Transitioning to a diet that accommodates specific health needs doesn't have to be an overnight overhaul. Gradual changes can make the process less overwhelming. Start by altering one meal a day or adjusting a single recipe each week. This slower pace allows you to adjust your palate and find replacements that you enjoy.

Keeping It Enjoyable

It's crucial that dietary changes remain enjoyable, which encourages consistency and long-term adherence. Try new recipes regularly, experiment with different spices and flavors, and invite friends or family to taste-test your creations. Food is a joyous part of life, and maintaining this joy can motivate you to stick with healthier habits.

Adapting recipes to suit specific health needs is a journey of discovery. It involves learning about your body's needs, experimenting with new ingredients, and tweaking traditional cooking methods. With creativity and a willingness to experiment, you can enjoy a diverse, flavorful, and healthy diet that supports your health goals. Remember, each small change you make contributes significantly to your overall well-being, allowing you to lead a healthier, more vibrant life.

CHAPTER 12:
Meal Planning and Preparation

Planning and preparing meals is essential for maintaining a healthy and balanced diet. By organizing your diet week, you can save time, reduce stress, and ensure you're consistently nourishing your body with wholesome foods.

ORGANIZING YOUR DIET WEEK

Setting Your Goals

The first step in meal planning is setting clear and achievable dietary goals. Whether your aim is weight management, improving energy levels, or supporting a specific health condition, having a defined goal will guide your food choices and meal structure. Consider what you want to achieve with your diet and tailor your meal plan to support these objectives.

Creating a Weekly Menu

Once you've established your goals, it's time to create a weekly menu. Start by selecting a variety of recipes that you enjoy and that align with your dietary needs. Balance is key – ensure your menu includes a mix of proteins, healthy fats, and carbohydrates, along with plenty of vegetables and fruits.

To keep things interesting and avoid monotony, choose recipes with different flavors and textures. For instance, mix up your protein sources by including poultry, fish, legumes, and plant-based options throughout the week. Incorporate seasonal produce to take advantage of the freshest and most nutritious ingredients available.

Planning Your Shopping List

A well-organized shopping list is crucial for efficient meal preparation. Once you've decided on your recipes, list all the ingredients you'll need. Group items by category – such as produce, dairy, meats, and pantry staples – to make your shopping trip quicker and more efficient. This approach helps ensure you have everything you need and reduces the likelihood of impulse purchases that don't align with your dietary goals.

Preparing in Advance

Meal preparation can significantly streamline your week. Set aside a specific time, such as Sunday afternoon, to prepare your meals. Cook in batches, making large quantities of dishes that can be easily reheated or used in different meals. For example, roast a variety of vegetables and cook a large batch of quinoa or brown rice to use in salads, bowls, and side dishes throughout the week.

Storing and Portioning

Proper storage and portioning are key to maintaining the freshness and nutritional value of your meals. Use airtight containers to store pre-cooked meals and ingredients in the refrigerator or freezer. Label containers with the date to keep track of freshness.

Consider portioning out meals into individual servings. This makes it easy to grab a balanced meal on busy days without having to measure or prepare additional ingredients. Pre-portioned snacks, such as cut vegetables, fruits, and nuts, are also convenient for maintaining healthy eating habits.

Staying Flexible

While planning is essential, it's also important to remain flexible. Life is unpredictable, and sometimes your schedule may change. Have a few quick and easy recipes or healthy convenience foods on hand for days when you don't have time to cook. This flexibility helps you stay on track with your dietary goals without feeling restricted.

Enjoying the Process

Finally, remember that meal planning and preparation should be enjoyable. Experiment with new recipes, involve family members in the process, and take pride in the healthy meals you create. This positive mindset will help you stay motivated and make meal planning a rewarding part of your lifestyle.

By organizing your diet week effectively, you set yourself up for success in maintaining a balanced and nutritious diet. With thoughtful planning, smart shopping, and efficient preparation, you can enjoy delicious meals that support your health and well-being every day.

28 DAYS MEAL PLAN

Week 1

Day	Breakfast	Lunch	Snack	Dinner	Dessert
Monday	Turkey and Spinach Omelette	Quinoa and Roasted Vegetable Salad	Almond and Date Energy Balls	Grilled Turkey Breast with Cauliflower Mash	Baked Apples with Cinnamon
Tuesday	Avocado and Berry Smoothie	Carrot and Ginger Soup	Celery Sticks with Almond Butter	Stuffed Bell Peppers with Quinoa and Vegetables	Dark Chocolate Avocado Mousse
Wednesday	Oatmeal with Turmeric and Almonds	Grilled Chicken with Quinoa and Steamed Vegetables	Green Detox Smoothie	Thai Beef Salad	Cashew Cheese with Figs
Thursday	Spinach, Flaxseed, and Blueberry Smoothie	Spinach and Walnut Salad with Citrus Vinaigrette	Pumpkin Seeds and Dried Cranberries	Seared Cod with Broccoli and Almonds	Mango and Coconut Rice
Friday	Greek Yogurt with Nuts and Honey	Tomato Basil Soup	Mixed Berry Salad	Eggplant and Tomato Stew	Almond Flour Lemon Cake
Saturday	Quinoa Porridge with Mixed Berries	Baked Salmon with Asparagus and Sweet Potatoes	Carrot and Beet Juice	Indian Chicken Curry with Cauliflower Rice	Banana Ice Cream
Sunday	Almond Butter and Banana Smoothie	Broccoli, Chickpea, and Avocado Salad	Sweet Potato and Beet Chips	Lemon Garlic Shrimp over Zucchini Noodles	Fruit Salad with Citrus Mint Dressing

Week 2

Day	Breakfast	Lunch	Snack	Dinner	Dessert
Monday	Cottage Cheese and Pineapple Bowl	Lentil and Spinach Soup	Cucumber and Hummus	Baked Sole with Lemon and Dill	Baked Peaches with Vanilla
Tuesday	Buckwheat with Honey and Cinnamon	Stir-Fried Tofu with Broccoli and Bell Peppers	Pineapple and Mint Juice	Moroccan Lentil Soup	Dairy-Free Raspberry Sorbet
Wednesday	Cucumber, Kale, and Apple Smoothie	Kale, Carrot, and Almond Salad	Walnut and Fig Bars	Lamb Chops with Mint Pesto	Grilled Pineapple with Honey and Lime
Thursday	Smoked Salmon and Avocado Toast	Chicken and Vegetable Broth	Sliced Apples with Peanut Butter	Turkey Lettuce Wraps	Coconut Flour Brownies
Friday	Millet Porridge with Apple and Flaxseeds	Shrimp and Avocado Wrap	Zucchini and Carrot Fritters	Japanese Miso Soup with Tofu	Pear and Vanilla Compote
Saturday	Chia Seed and Peach Smoothie	Pea and Mint Soup	Berry and Yogurt Smoothie	Baked Chicken with Brussels Sprouts	Peanut Butter Protein Balls
Sunday	Scrambled Eggs with Sautéed Mushrooms	Arugula, Fennel, and Orange Salad	Aloe Vera and Cucumber Juice	Spanish Gazpacho	Avocado Lime Cheesecake

Week 3

Day	Breakfast	Lunch	Snack	Dinner	Dessert
Monday	Barley Porridge with Dates and Cardamom	Mushroom and Thyme Soup	Protein-Packed Trail Mix	Tuna Salad with Avocado	Strawberry and Basil Sorbet
Tuesday	Coconut Water and Pineapple Smoothie	Portobello Mushroom Steak	Roasted Chickpeas with Sea Salt	Italian Zucchini Pasta	Flourless Chocolate Chip Cookies
Wednesday	Grilled Chicken Sausage with Tomato Salsa	Veggie and Quinoa Stuffed Peppers	Watermelon and Basil Smoothie	Herb-Roasted Pork Tenderloin	Almond Milk Rice Pudding
Thursday	Amaranth Porridge with Cherry and Walnut	Lentil Salad with Cucumber and Mint	Bell Pepper Strips with Guacamole	Grilled Asparagus and Poached Egg	Baked Apples with Cinnamon
Friday	Celery and Green Apple Smoothie	Butternut Squash Soup	Hard-Boiled Eggs with Spinach Dip	Caprese Salad with Balsamic Reduction	Lemon and Blueberry Bar
Saturday	Turkey and Spinach Omelette	Baked Trout with Lemon and Dill	Pumpkin Seeds and Dried Cranberries	Beef and Broccoli Stir Fry	Frozen Yogurt with Honey and Almonds
Sunday	Oatmeal with Turmeric and Almonds	Spicy Pumpkin Soup	Pineapple and Mint Juice	Chickpea and Spinach Curry	Coconut Tapioca Pudding

Week 4

Day	Breakfast	Lunch	Snack	Dinner	Dessert
Monday	Spinach, Flaxseed, and Blueberry Smoothie	Grilled Chicken with Quinoa and Steamed Vegetables	Sliced Apples with Peanut Butter	Greek Stuffed Tomatoes	Almond Flour Lemon Cake
Tuesday	Tofu Scramble with Spinach and Peppers	Broccoli, Chickpea, and Avocado Salad	Carrot and Beet Juice	Spicy Grilled Tuna Steaks	Grilled Pineapple with Honey and Lime
Wednesday	Millet Porridge with Apple and Flaxseeds	Beef Stew with Root Vegetables	Cottage Cheese with Sliced Peaches	Stuffed Bell Peppers with Quinoa and Vegetables	Dark Chocolate Avocado Mousse
Thursday	Egg White Frittata with Asparagus	Chicken and Vegetable Broth	Mixed Berry Salad	Baked Sole with Lemon and Dill	Banana Ice Cream
Friday	Amaranth Porridge with Cherry and Walnut	Spinach and Walnut Salad with Citrus Vinaigrette	Zucchini and Carrot Fritters	Lamb Chops with Mint Pesto	Baked Peaches with Vanilla
Saturday	Cucumber, Kale, and Apple Smoothie	Veggie and Quinoa Stuffed Peppers	Pomegranate and Lime Juice	Japanese Miso Soup with Tofu	Vegan Chocolate Gelato
Sunday	Baked Eggs in Avocado Cups	Carrot and Ginger Soup	Green Detox Smoothie	Indian Chicken Curry with Cauliflower Rice	Avocado Lime Cheesecake

CHAPTER 13:
Maintaining Your Diet and Motivation

Sticking to a healthy diet can sometimes feel challenging, especially when life gets busy or when temptations arise. However, maintaining your diet and staying motivated is crucial for achieving your health goals. This chapter will provide you with practical strategies for overcoming dietary challenges and staying motivated. Additionally, we'll explore the benefits of engaging with the Galveston Diet community for support and inspiration.

OVERCOMING DIETARY CHALLENGES

One of the first steps in overcoming dietary challenges is identifying what they are. Common obstacles include time constraints, cravings, social pressures, and emotional eating. Recognizing these challenges early on can help you develop strategies to address them effectively.

A busy schedule can make it difficult to prepare healthy meals. To combat this, consider meal prepping on weekends or on a day when you have more free time. Preparing meals in advance ensures you have healthy options ready to go, even on the busiest days.

Cravings for unhealthy foods can derail your diet. Instead of giving in, find healthier alternatives that satisfy your cravings. For instance, if you're craving something sweet, reach for a piece of fruit or a small serving of dark chocolate. Keeping healthy snacks on hand can also help curb cravings.

Social events often involve food and drinks that may not align with your dietary goals. Plan ahead by eating a healthy meal before attending events or bringing a nutritious dish to share. Don't be afraid to communicate your dietary preferences with friends and family – they will likely support your commitment to a healthier lifestyle.

Emotional eating can be a significant barrier to maintaining a healthy diet. When you feel stressed, anxious, or upset, find alternative ways to cope. Exercise, meditation, or engaging in a hobby can help you manage emotions without turning to food.

Maintaining a positive mindset is essential for long-term success. Focus on the benefits of your diet, such as improved energy levels, better mood, and overall health. Celebrate small victories and milestones along the way to keep yourself motivated. Remember, it's not about perfection but about making consistent, healthier choices.

Setting realistic and achievable goals is key to maintaining motivation. Break down your overall health objectives into smaller, manageable steps. For example, instead of aiming to lose a large amount of weight quickly, focus on losing a few pounds each month. This approach makes your goals more attainable and less overwhelming.

ENGAGING WITH THE GALVESTON DIET COMMUNITY

Engaging with a community of like-minded individuals can provide invaluable support and inspiration. The Galveston Diet community is filled with people who share similar health goals and challenges. Connecting with others can help you stay motivated and provide a sense of camaraderie.

Online communities, such as forums, social media groups, and dedicated websites, offer a platform to share experiences, recipes, and tips. Participating in these groups allows you to ask questions, seek advice, and celebrate successes with others who understand your journey. These interactions can be incredibly encouraging, especially on days when you might feel discouraged.

Look for local groups or events related to the Galveston Diet. These might include cooking classes, health seminars, or workout groups. Attending in-person events can help you build a network of supportive friends and provide opportunities to learn more about healthy living.

Sharing your successes with the community can be highly motivating. When you achieve a milestone or overcome a challenge, share your story. Your experiences can inspire others and reinforce your commitment to your diet. Plus, receiving positive feedback and encouragement from others can boost your confidence and motivation.

The Galveston Diet community is a treasure trove of knowledge and experience. Take advantage of the collective wisdom by learning from others. Whether it's new recipes, meal prep tips, or strategies for dealing with cravings, there's always something new to discover. Engaging with the community helps you stay informed and inspired.

PRACTICAL TIPS FOR STAYING MOTIVATED

Tracking Your Progress

Keeping track of your progress is an effective way to stay motivated. Use a journal, app, or calendar to record your meals, exercise, and any changes you notice in your health. Reviewing your progress regularly can remind you of how far you've come and encourage you to keep going.

Rewarding Yourself

Rewarding yourself for sticking to your diet can provide additional motivation. Choose non-food rewards that you enjoy, such as a relaxing spa day, a new book, or a fun outing. Rewards give you something to look forward to and celebrate your hard work and dedication.

Staying Flexible

While it's important to stick to your diet, it's also crucial to stay flexible. Life is unpredictable, and there will be times when you might stray from your plan. Instead of feeling guilty, acknowledge it and get back on track with your next meal. Flexibility helps you maintain a healthy relationship with food and reduces stress.

Continuing Education

Education is a powerful tool for motivation. Continuously learn about nutrition, health, and the benefits of the Galveston Diet. Understanding the science behind your dietary choices can reinforce your commitment and provide new ideas for maintaining a healthy lifestyle.

Creating a Supportive Environment

Your environment plays a significant role in your dietary success. Surround yourself with supportive people and remove temptations from your home. Stock your kitchen with healthy foods and keep your living space organized to reduce stress. A supportive environment makes it easier to stay on track and maintain your motivation.

Finding Joy in the Process

Lastly, find joy in the process of maintaining your diet. Experiment with new recipes, savor your meals, and appreciate the positive changes in your health. When you enjoy what you're doing, it becomes less of a chore and more of a fulfilling part of your life.

Maintaining your diet and staying motivated is a continuous process that requires dedication and support. By overcoming dietary challenges, engaging with the Galveston Diet community, and implementing practical tips, you can achieve your health goals and enjoy a vibrant, healthy life. Remember, it's about making consistent, healthy choices and finding joy in the journey toward better health.

CONCLUSION

Adopting the Galveston Diet is more than just following a set of guidelines; it's about committing to a lifestyle that fosters long-term health and well-being. As we wrap up this guide, it's important to reflect on the principles and practices that will sustain your commitment to this healthy way of living. The journey may have its challenges, but the rewards—improved health, increased energy, and a more balanced life—are well worth the effort.

One of the keys to sustaining the Galveston Diet is making it an integral part of your daily routine. This involves more than just meal planning and preparation; it's about developing habits that align with the diet's principles. Start each day with a nutritious breakfast, plan balanced meals, and incorporate healthy snacks to keep your energy levels stable. By making these practices routine, they become second nature.

As you progress with the Galveston Diet, continue to set new health goals. Whether it's increasing your physical activity, improving your sleep habits, or learning new recipes, having goals keeps you focused and motivated. Celebrate each milestone, no matter how small, and use it as a stepping stone toward your next achievement.

Find joy in discovering new recipes, savoring delicious meals, and experiencing the positive changes in your health. When you enjoy what you're doing, it becomes a rewarding part of your life rather than a chore. Remember to take time to appreciate the journey and the improvements in your well-being.

Regularly assess your progress and adjust your approach as needed. This involves checking in with yourself to see how you're feeling, evaluating the effectiveness of your meal plans, and making changes to better suit your needs. Self-assessment helps you stay aligned with your goals and ensures that you continue to progress in a healthy and balanced manner.

Complement your diet with regular physical activity. Exercise not only supports weight management but also enhances mood, energy levels, and overall health. Find activities you enjoy, whether it's walking, yoga, swimming, or strength training, and make them a regular part of your routine. Consistency in physical activity, just like in diet, plays a crucial role in maintaining long-term health benefits.

Maintaining a healthy lifestyle is a marathon, not a sprint. It's important to stay positive and patient, especially during times when progress seems slow. Trust the process and remain committed to your goals. Positive changes in health take time, and consistency will ultimately lead to lasting results.

AUTHOR'S ACKNOWLEDGEMENTS

Writing this book and sharing the principles of the Galveston Diet has been a deeply fulfilling experience. It wouldn't have been possible without the support, inspiration, and encouragement of many individuals and communities. I am profoundly grateful to everyone who has been a part of this journey.

First and foremost, I want to thank my family and friends who have been my constant source of support. Your understanding and encouragement have been invaluable. Thank you for your patience as I spent countless hours researching, writing, and testing recipes. Your love and support mean the world to me.

To my readers, thank you for choosing this book and for your commitment to a healthier lifestyle. Your journey is an inspiration, and I am honored to be a part of it. I hope the recipes, tips, and insights shared in this book help you achieve your health goals and enjoy a vibrant, balanced life.

Writing this book has been a collaborative effort, and I am deeply grateful to everyone who has supported and inspired me along the way. Together, we can continue to promote health and well-being, one delicious meal at a time. Thank you for being a part of this journey.

Made in the USA
Monee, IL
12 November 2024

69929055R00057